THE DESIRES OF YOUR HEART

THE DESIRES OF YOUR HEART

TOM GARDNER

Foursquare Media

THE DESIRES OF YOUR HEART by Tom Gardner
Published by Foursquare Media
1910 W. Sunset Blvd., Suite 200
Los Angeles, California 90026

This book is produced and distributed by Creation House, a part of Strang Communications, www.creationhouse.com.

Cover design by Terry Clifton

Library of Congress Control Number: 2007924910
International Standard Book Number: 978-1-59979-080-0

First Edition

07 08 09 10 11 — 987654321
Printed in the United States of America

ACKNOWLEDGMENTS

Many thanks to:

§ My parents, for being great examples of stewardship

§ My Sunshine Hills family, for believing in a young man with lots of ideas

§ My family and friends who read and reread the countless drafts of this book

§ Wanda Brackett, for being an advocate of this project

§ Jerry Cook, for his encouragement and help in "zipping up" my writing

§ My wife, Lottie, and my four daughters who released me to follow my dream to write this book

§ My editor, Larry Libby, for helping me make my message more readable

CONTENTS

FOREWORD

THE SUBJECT OF money in the church world is loaded
with emotion, legalism, fear, non-sense, and borderline
religious magic. Tom Gardner is an articulate, clear-
thinking Christian leader who courageously cuts through the
brush and helps us take another look. His practical insights and
common sense applications on this important biblical theme are
a refreshing contribution.

I have enjoyed Tom's friendship and seen the positive effects
of his ministry for many years. This book is not theoretical, but
describes the principles by which he and his family consistently
live. When a man's life illustrates his theology, he deserves a
serious hearing. Tom has earned that hearing. You will be glad
you listened.

—JERRY COOK
AUTHOR OF *LOVE, ACCEPTANCE, AND FORGIVENESS*

PREFACE

THE DESIRES OF *Your Heart*—what an odd name for a book on giving! You might expect a title like that on a book about love and marriage—but giving?

In fact, this is a book about loving God and putting Him first. It's also a book about God loving us and His intention to give us the desires of our hearts.

This isn't a book about managing money; it's a book about managing life. How you think about and handle money makes a strong statement about your view of life, and life's priorities.

We were created as eternal beings, and no matter what Madison Avenue and all those ads on radio and TV tell us, the things that truly satisfy our hearts are intangibles. People may think they need a bigger house and an SUV, but what we're really looking for is love and a purpose for living. We want to feel a sense of fulfillment, of significance. We want to give ourselves to something beyond ourselves. Somewhere deep within we know that the toys and trinkets of earth are fleeting and won't last. Only the things of eternity will stand the test of time.

The heart is a person's very center—the core and substance of who we really are. And the desires of our heart are all about those things that we truly value, not just the things we say we value.

How do you discover the secret of finding the desires of your heart, the "pearl of great price"?

By delighting yourself in the Lord.

Then, and only then, can God give you the desires of your heart. Why? Because your desires will be His desires.

As you learn the secret of putting Him first in your life, you will start to understand that you own nothing and He owns everything. He has entrusted the resources of His kingdom into your care for one purpose—to see His lost children restored and His purposes fulfilled.

The Central Question

The writing of this book grew out of two separate experiences. The first was someone challenging my belief system. Is tithing, giving back to the Lord ten percent of our income, really a commandment?

To be honest, I hadn't given the matter much thought. I had just accepted what I had always been taught. All of my Christian life I had believed that tithing certainly *was* a commandment. A Christian had an obligation to tithe in obedience to God's command.

This worked for me until I began to encounter people who raised some very legitimate questions—questions for which I had no answer. These weren't people looking for an excuse not to give to the Lord's work; they really wanted to know what the Bible said.

How would I respond?

The second experience grew out of serving as a pastor to people who truly wanted to honor God with their giving, but had no idea where to begin.

Asking questions is always a good place to begin. Good teachers give people freedom to ask legitimate questions without fear of criticism or rebuke. Jesus was such a teacher. When someone asked a good question, Jesus' answer encouraged the questioner to think in a new way.

And that's positive. It's healthy to examine our beliefs. The process helps us separate the message from the methods, truth from tradition. Examination helps us to "know what we know."

So it was for me. My examination of these questions gave birth to even more questions.

Is tithing really a commandment (obligatory) or is it a principle (voluntary) of God's kingdom?

What does the Bible actually say on the subject?

If what I had believed at an earlier time was somehow invalid, what were the implications for me—someone who gets paid because people tithe? What were the implications for the church? How was the work of the ministry to be funded?

It had always troubled me that the church had to go back to the Old Testament to prove that tithing is a command. After all, if believers are required to keep *some* of the 613 commandments, who decides which ones are still binding? We may find ourselves keeping the commandments we like and ignoring the ones we don't.

The simple truth is that our walk with Jesus Christ touches every area of daily life. This includes understanding what God teaches about money and its place in our priority systems. God cares about every aspect of our lives because He loves us and wants what's best for us. He desires for us to prosper, and this prosperity is so much more than earthly wealth. In fact, He wants to lavish upon us the incalculable riches of His Kingdom. (See Luke 12:32–33.)

My central purpose for writing this book is to show how giving tithes and offerings is an integral part of our worship to God.

But even before I wrote the first word in this book, I was certain of one thing: tithing or not tithing has nothing to do with our salvation. Zero. It does, however, have everything to do with our *fruitfulness*. Our view of money has a direct bearing on our daily relationship with God.

Will we put Him first?

Truth for the Heart

One of the very first scriptures I learned in Sunday School was Psalm 37:4: "Delight yourself in the LORD and he will give you the desires of your heart." Serving God and putting Him first should never be a "chore," but a delight. When loving becomes difficult, something is wrong—very wrong. Right from the beginning, worshiping and loving God were meant to bring joy.

Honoring God with our material substance is truth for the heart more than for the head. Head knowledge is based on arguments and information. Heart knowledge is based upon love and conviction that God is both willing and able to provide for our needs.

Heart is the substance of relationship. When you have to create rules to govern human behavior, there can never be enough. Human conduct is best governed from the inside. Following God is all about heart.

And so is this book.

CHAPTER 1

A MATTER OF THE HEART

Money makes people funny.

—OREST HERSHICK

EXPERIENCED WHITEWATER RAFTERS always pay very careful attention to warning signs posted along the riverbank. Missing such signs, or simply ignoring them, could cost you your life. One of the signs you always want to respect says, "Warning! Boaters Exit River Here. Falls Ahead."

Rafters and canoers know that sign means to paddle for shore as fast and hard as you possibly can. If you don't, if you shrug your shoulders, if you let yourself become caught in the current, it will be too late to turn back.

The apostle Paul posted such a warning sign in the New Testament book of 1 Timothy. He wrote to his young disciple:

> People who want to get rich fall into temptation and a trap and into many foolish and harmful desires that plunge men into ruin and destruction. For the love of money is a root of all kinds of evil. Some people, eager for money, have wandered from the faith and pierced themselves with many griefs. But you, man of God, flee from all this.
>
> —1 TIMOTHY 6:9–11

Many people through the years—perhaps most people—have heard a distortion of those words. They understood the Bible to say, "Money is the root of all evil." But that's not what Paul said. The apostle wrote, "The love of money is a root of all kinds of evil."

It's a warning sign on the river keeping boaters away from the deadly falls just around the corner. Paul cautions Timothy—and all who would read this scripture down through the millennia—to be very careful, very prudent about money and possessions. Those who ignore that caution will pay the very heavy price that he describes.

There's the fall into temptation.

There's the trap.

There are the waterfalls that "plunge men into ruin and destruction."

But here's the surprise. The trap isn't money. Money is neutral, an integral part of the economic system of this world. Money is simply a basic fact of life. The trap is the love of money—and what it does to the human soul.

Orest Hershick was an influential friend in my life. By most anyone's definition, he was what one would call a high roller. Orest grew up in the small Canadian town of Prince Albert, Saskatchewan, and made a lot of money in his lifetime. He also lost a lot of money. This man who had owned car dealerships and professional hockey teams ended up with two dollars to his name on the front lawn of his daughter's house with nowhere else to go.

Orest's daughter, however, was a believer. Putting aside the hurt her father had caused her through the years, she accepted him into her life once more. Through this undeserved kindness (and a host of other supernatural events), Orest made the best decision of his life. He invited Jesus Christ to become his Savior and Lord.

My friend never regained his earthly wealth. Before he died of cancer, however, I asked him if he would trade Jesus for what he had once possessed.

"Not on your life," he told me. Then he shook his head, sighed deeply, and said, "Pastor Tom, money makes people funny."

Coming to Grips

There's no dodging the money issue. We must all come to grips with the realities of money and possessions and the place they hold in our lives. Our philosophy of money grows out of our philosophy of life.

Everyone has a philosophy of life—a system of beliefs that helps them organize how they live and what they think is true. Some people have given serious thought to such a philosophy and some have not, but everyone operates under a system of guiding principles—even if that principle is "do nothing and take life as it comes."

The same is true of money and possessions. Some have given a great deal of thought to these issues, and others have scarcely considered them at all. Whether thought out or not, however, everyone has a philosophy of money. The challenge for believers is to develop a philosophy that's biblical and that works.

Even though our attitude toward money and possessions plays a critical, pivotal role in our lives, many pastors and Christian leaders tend to tiptoe around the whole subject—or avoid it entirely—for fear of offending people. It's every pastor's dilemma: people need to understand what the Bible has to say about money (and it's a lot), but no one wants to be manipulated, badgered, or lectured.

It was a dilemma for me, too. I had spoken on numerous Bible passages that touched on the subject of our possessions, but I had mostly steered away from doing anything comprehensive.

It was my wife who challenged me to rethink that practice.

She pointed out my responsibility as the shepherd to lead the people and to help them understand the ways of God. This certainly included teaching them what God has to say about money, material goods, and the responsibility to be a faithful steward.

She was right. If people in positions of spiritual maturity and influence fail to give instruction on matters of great importance, they forfeit their leadership, abandoning their followers to form their own opinions from a hodge-podge of sources that may not be reliable.

The lack of teaching on the subject of good money management isn't limited to the church. Many people never receive instruction at home on handling money wisely. As with the subject of sexuality, parents make the dangerous assumption that their children will just "pick up what they need to know" over the course of time. They shirk their role as parents to train and equip their offspring to be accountable, responsible adults, assuming the kids will glean the information elsewhere. Maybe at school. Or at church. Or from someone else—anyone else.

These parents are right. Young people will pick up information and begin to form their own attitudes, opinions, and lifelong habits. But what they learn may be far, far afield from God's best for their lives.

An essential part of raising children and making disciples is helping them understand that money, when used correctly and in keeping with God's principles, has the ability to create wonderful possibilities.

A Matter of the Heart

My introduction to honoring God with my money came at an early age. My parents ingrained in me the principle of tithing. They taught me that ten percent of what I received belonged to God. A nickel of my fifty-cents weekly allowance went to Jesus.

No, God didn't need my nickel. But He wanted my heart, and He wanted me to acknowledge His ownership of all that I had.

Tithing, then, has been a lifelong reality in my life. I tithe because I acknowledge God's ownership, and He has proven Himself faithful to me in ways far beyond my understanding or ability to express. I have no doubt that I'm far better off financially—and in every other way—than I would have been, had I trusted in my own abilities.

The Bible clearly and indisputably teaches that a worshiper of God is to be a giver. When God has your heart, He has your wallet too. The opposite of this is not true. The church may have a hold on people's wallets, but not necessarily their hearts. Pressuring people to give out of guilt and manipulation does not bring joy to the giver; it produces bitterness.

First and foremost, we need to cultivate within us the heart of Christ, who saw people lost and without hope. (See Matthew 9:35–38.) Our emphasis should be on making disciples of Christ, rather than having more tithers in our churches. When people come to know Jesus personally, they will then be open to living their lives in a way that pleases Him and in a way that He can bless. As they learn to move through their days in accordance with God's Word, they see how obedience brings blessing in their lives and the lives of those they touch. They, in turn, want to bless others. People give of their resources, including their money, to see others come to know Christ.

Many people have been taught that life as a believer is one of grim endurance and that God's will is always difficult. Instead of experiencing the truth that sets them free, they buy into the lie that following God brings them into bondage. Granted, obedience can sometimes be very difficult. Obeying God means saying "no" to our selfish desires. On the other hand, living a life in obedience to God's laws brings a life of fulfillment and fruitfulness that's simply not possible by living any other way.

Money and Happiness

In February of 2004, Mel Gibson created quite a stir with the release of his movie, *The Passion of the Christ*. During the weeks before and after the graphic movie hit theaters worldwide, Gibson's reasons for making the film became the topic of scores of interviews and articles.

In an interview with ABC journalist Diane Sawyer, Gibson unabashedly stated that he'd had all that Hollywood and this world had to offer: fame, wealth, pleasure, and a life of ease. He told all who would listen that those things did not—could not—bring him happiness. There comes a time, he said, when you ask yourself, "Is this all there is?" That's when a person looks up to heaven and pleads, "If there is a God, please help."[1]

Remembering his Catholic roots, Gibson passionately gave himself to portraying the sacrificial death of Jesus. The actor-director told Sawyer that remembering what Jesus had suffered brought healing to his soul.

Money cannot buy happiness or health or eternal life. Money or, more correctly, the pursuit of earthly wealth and power, can bring great heartache.

Remember King Midas? He was the fairy-tale king who received a magical "gift": Everything he touched turned to gold. The "Midas touch" became a nightmare, however, when that fabled touch turned his own beloved little daughter—so full of warmth and love—into the cold, unfeeling metal. King Midas found out quickly, and too late, what was really important in life.

Life is so much more than money.

Money Is Spiritual

Make no mistake: money is spiritual. It has power and influence far beyond the material world. In fact, even as you read these words, money is flowing all around you. (Stay with me here!) On any given day, billions and billions of invisible dollars fly through the air by electronic means without anyone actually seeing or touching any actual currency. Still, people put their faith in such transfers and transactions.

Because money is spiritual, it shouldn't surprise us that Jesus actually had quite a bit to say on the subject. He taught that we were to be "in" the world and not "of" the world. (See John 17.) Possessing a physical body, we inhabit the time/space continuum we call life. Living in this world as we do, we're part of the present economic system. We are not, however, to live our lives as a part of this fallen world system, flawed by sin and ruled by the god of this world.

We've all heard people swear up and down that if they became rich it wouldn't change them.

Well, maybe and maybe not.

One of the writers of the book of Proverbs worried about that very thing, asking the Lord to give him no more than what he required for his daily needs. (See Proverbs 30:8.) And why was that? Because evidently he knew himself. And he knew that his heart couldn't really be trusted with sudden prosperity.

He wrote, "Otherwise, I may have too much and disown you and say, 'Who is the LORD?'" (Prov. 30:9).

It's a wise man who knows his limits—and so few of us do.

The love of money, of course, isn't restricted to the wealthy. People with very little money at all can actually be more bound up in the area of finances than the rich. They become obsessed, spending their waking hours thinking about what they don't have and how they might gain more. Money can easily become an idol for any of us.

I really like the following quotation: "Money is simply something that God entrusts to us and allows us to use during our lifetime."[2] Sweet and simple. God owns everything; we own nothing. He has entrusted us with His riches so we can further His purposes here on earth.

Money Is a Tool

Tools allow us to do things we otherwise couldn't do. I can't pull a nail out of a board or loosen the lug nut on a car wheel with my bare hands. However, I can easily perform either of these tasks with the right tool. Things like claw hammers and wrenches expand the capability of the human hand.

So it is with money. Money makes it possible to do things we couldn't otherwise do, and stewardship simply means that we take care of that "power tool," maintaining it so it will be there when we need it next. As with any other tool, money needs to be understood and used skillfully. A powerful force for good, money can just as quickly become a force that will pull down a marriage, a family, a home, or a church.

Money, then, is a means to an end and not an end in itself.

Two Extremes

The concept or principle of stewardship is not immune from the attacks of the Father of Lies. (See John 8:44.) Satan will do everything he can to twist the truth concerning money and its place in our lives.

❦   He *wants* to see marriages fail.

❦   He *wants* to see families shattered.

❦   He *wants* to see friendships alienated.

❦   He *wants* to bend and warp every good gift God has ever intended for us.

This twisting technique of Satan often finds its expression through a play on opposites. On most any major issue we face in life, we find ourselves between two tension points. Success in our lives is all about finding the balance between those two poles. When it comes to stewardship, the two extremes are (1) caring too much about the future, and (2) not caring enough.

"Why are you so concerned about your finances? Don't you trust God?"

Have you ever heard that one? Sometimes people who pay close attention to good stewardship principles get labeled as "tight." Or "uptight."

This underscores the fundamental confusion between our part and God's part. We are called into *partnership* with God. He will do His part to provide for our basic needs, because He is faithful and true. We need to do our part by being obedient, diligently practicing the principles of good stewardship.

That means a reasonable and prudent attention to detail.

On the other hand, some carry that attention over the edge. They become overly worried about the future and about having enough to meet any future need. They become anxious and sometimes find themselves overtaken by the poverty spirit that says, "There is never enough." Such worry can cause people to be stingy, withholding their tithes and offerings.

The steady creep of materialism can overtake anyone. Here's what Proverbs 11:24–26 has to say on this matter:

> One man gives freely, yet gains even more; another withholds unduly, but comes to poverty. A generous man will prosper; he who refreshes others will himself be refreshed. People curse the man who hoards grain, but blessing crowns him who is willing to sell.

At another extreme, a strong message of our present society is "You only live once, so grab all the gusto you can." People who have no concept of eternity easily fall into an "easy come; easy go" attitude. Believers can get caught in this trap as well.

The Real Issue

At the very root of this discussion is a little four-letter word.

Self.

For the Christian, the word *self* is a way of describing the real you, the person you are on the inside. The Bible also refers to the *self* as our fallen nature: the part that is at odds with God and thinks only of what's good for itself.

As Christians, we believe that every human being is born with a fallen nature. Romans 5:12 shows us that we have all received this fallen or sin nature through Adam's original sin. The struggle between the flesh and the spirit, the desire to please God and simultaneously please our selfishness, is a major theme of Paul's writings. Our fallen nature has a very strong self-preservation instinct that wants to make sure its needs are taken care of—to the exclusion of everyone else. This gets translated into our contemporary society as "looking out for number one."

Our self or flesh is also proud. It doesn't like to acknowledge any other king. Any discussion about self, then, is really about who is the lord of your life. Ask yourself, "Who's really in charge? Who is it that I worship: God or myself?"

That's the crux of the issue.

That's the crux of life.

Tithing acknowledges a power and authority outside of self by recognizing a Source greater than ourselves. In our arrogance we find it hard to believe that someone, in this case Almighty God, will really meet our needs and take care of us. We're so conditioned to look after our own needs that we find it difficult to believe that God really cares and has promised to provide for us.

There Must Be a Hitch

And so there is a hitch. We must surrender control of our very lives to Him, fully trusting in Him and in His goodness.

CHAPTER 2

PORTRAIT OF A STEWARD

The more God gives you, the more responsible he expects you to be.

—RICK WARREN[1]

A STEWARD IS ONE who has been entrusted with the resources of another. While not the owner, a steward does business in the owner's name, remaining accountable for the security and increase of that investment.

Stewards stand in stark contrast to consumers. Consumers use up resources; stewards take care of the resources given them.

Stewardship flows through the pages of Scripture like a repeating musical refrain in a symphony. The Bible narrative assumes throughout that followers of God both understand and practice stewardship.

And the teaching begins at the very beginning.

Literally.

Created for Stewardship

In the beginning God created the heavens and the earth.

—GENESIS 1:1

This very first verse of the Bible establishes God's creation and ownership of all things. King David picked up on this majestic theme in one of his psalms:

> The earth is the LORD's, and everything in it, the world, and all who live in it.
>
> —PSALM 24:1

Creation is God's handiwork, and the care of that creation was His to give. As owner of all, God placed Adam and Eve in the Garden of Eden as stewards. The Creator trusted Adam, His representative and trustee, to take care of the creation and see it flourish, all the while enjoying the increase.

Mankind was not the owner of earth. Mankind has never been the owner of earth.

Instead, our first father and mother were charged with the responsibility of managing God's world. "Be fruitful," God said to them, "and increase in number; fill the earth and subdue it" (Gen. 1:28).

We have failed in our responsibility as stewards over our world. Fouling our own nest, we must now deal with the ravages of pollution and the results of not respecting the laws of nature, all in the name of expansion and meeting our immediate perceived needs.

Instead of being good stewards, we have been consumers. Those two words have little in common. In fact, they are opposites. A consumer uses up what he has, giving little thought to the future. A steward is a conserver, refusing to abuse or waste what he has been given to manage.

Consumerism drives our economy and plays on our insecurities. We buy into the lie that all of our problems will be solved if we drive the right car or wear the right brand of jeans, reinforcing the mistaken idea that happiness and fulfillment come from material things.

The story Jesus told in Matthew 25:14–29 contains a simple but powerful summary of what it means to be a good steward:

> Again, it will be like a man going on a journey, who called his servants and entrusted his property to them. To one he gave five talents of money, to another two talents, and to another one talent, each according to his ability. Then he went on his journey. The man who had received the five talents went at once and put his money to work and gained five more. So also, the one with the two talents gained two more. But the man who had received the one talent went off, dug a hole in the ground and hid his master's money.
>
> After a long time the master of those servants returned and settled accounts with them. The man who had received the five talents brought the other five. "Master," he said, "you entrusted me with five talents. See, I have gained five more."
>
> His master replied, "Well done, good and faithful servant! You have been faithful with a few things; I will put you in charge of many things. Come and share your master's happiness!"
>
> The man with the two talents also came. "Master," he said, "you entrusted me with two talents; see, I have gained two more."
>
> His master replied, "Well done, good and faithful servant! You have been faithful with a few things; I will put you in charge of many things. Come and share your master's happiness!"
>
> Then the man who had received the one talent came. "Master," he said, "I knew that you are a hard man, harvesting where you have not sown and gathering where you have not scattered seed. So I was afraid and went out and hid your talent in the ground. See, here is what belongs to you."

His master replied, "You wicked, lazy servant! So you knew that I harvest where I have not sown and gather where I have not scattered seed? Well then, you should have put my money on deposit with the bankers, so that when I returned I would have received it back with interest.

"Take the talent from him and give it to the one who has the ten talents. For everyone who has will be given more, and he will have an abundance. Whoever does not have, even what he has will be taken from him."

Even a quick read-through of our Lord's story reveals several significant facts:

ᔓ   All three stewards had the very same master.

ᔓ   The master distributed to each one according to his assessment of the steward's ability.

ᔓ   The first two servants understood the concept of stewardship and put their talents to use, resulting in an increase.

ᔓ   The first two stewards received identical commendations from the master.

ᔓ   The last steward, deceived by a warped and inaccurate view of the master, hid his talent. Instead of a commendation, he received a severe rebuke.

Here are a few of the principles taught in this story:

ᔓ   Good stewardship causes talents and abilities to increase.

♪ Talents and abilities grow with use.

♪ Poor stewardship causes even what we have to be lost.

♪ Talents and abilities decrease with neglect. What we don't use we lose.

As you can see from this story told by Jesus, stewardship includes, but goes far beyond, finances. It encompasses all that is entrusted into our care while on earth. God asks that we be good stewards of everything. Rick Warren says, "Our time on earth and our energy, intelligence, opportunities, relationships, and resources are all gifts from God that he has entrusted to our care and management. We are stewards of whatever God gives us."[2]

Stewardship takes into account that good management of financial resources is but a part of the greater whole. All too often, however, the organized church puts its emphasis on the care and handling of money to the exclusion of all else.

In reality, stewardship is a way of life.

Stewardship and Worship

Being a steward is an inseparable part of our worship. Our English word is related to *worthship*, ascribing worth to something or someone. Worship, like stewardship, is part of the ebb and flow of daily life, not just an activity.

Does music lift us into the presence of God?

Then so does stewardship!

Worship is so much more than the joy, goose bumps, and spiritual feel-goods of an inspiring hour of music and singing. In fact, worship is, and has always been, about sacrifice. In the Old

Testament era people brought physical sacrifices to present to the Lord as acts of reverence and devotion. These sacrifices were never intended to be an end in themselves, but a tangible representation that sin always costs something.

Worship is all about sacrifice. And so is stewardship. We offer ourselves as living sacrifices to the Lord, and all that we have is His. (See Romans 12:1–2.)

Stewarding people

The use or abuse of material things has its own consequences. When things are used up, they are used up, and that's that. When we use people up, we damage an eternal being created in the image of God.

The idea of accountability is fundamental to stewardship, and giving an account applies to everything—including how we deal with people. A consumer mentality may be destructive when it comes to material things, but it is deadly when applied to people. The writer of Hebrews says, "Obey your leaders and submit to their authority. They keep watch over you as men who must give an account. Obey them so that their work will be a joy, not a burden, for that would be of no advantage to you" (Heb. 13:17). Christian leaders are stewards of those they lead, and will one day stand before Almighty God and answer for their treatment of those entrusted to their care.

Significantly, pastors are also referred to as shepherds. John 10 records Jesus' teaching that the shepherd lives for the sheep; the sheep do not exist for the shepherd. Contemporary Christian leaders need to follow the model of stewardship demonstrated by Jesus, the Good Shepherd, and not the bad example of shepherds who fleece the sheep for their own selfish ends. (See Ezekiel 34:2–16.)

Stewardship and tithing

The principle of tithing isn't some magic pill that reverses our fortunes and brings in prosperity like the spring rains. Life doesn't suddenly come up roses just because we put ten percent of our income into the offering. Tithing must be part of the overall good stewardship of all resources entrusted into our management.

Some pastors and Christian teachers with access to the Media have twisted the Scriptures, leading people to believe that as long as they tithe, God will guarantee material abundance in return. The truth is, God *does* want to bless us—in every way—and the Bible clearly demonstrates the relationship between receiving, honoring God, and enjoying His bounty. Nowhere does the Bible guarantee that all believers in Christ, including those who tithe, will be wealthy in a material sense. What then has God promised? "That He will supply our needs." (See Philippians 4:19.)

People may give ten percent of their income, but squander ninety percent. That's not good stewardship. Those who live in this manner can't blame God when things don't go well for them.

The decision to tithe helps us along the road to good stewardship, because we're forced to take a hard look at our priorities and become better managers of that which God has entrusted to us. That's a blessing in itself! Coming face to face with our real values and priorities—difficult or painful as that may be on occasion—is one of the most valuable encounters we can ever experience.

A many-splendored thing

Throughout the pages of the Bible, the Holy Spirit underlines a multitude of behaviors associated with good stewardship.

Diligence

> Watch over your heart with all diligence, For from it flow the springs of life.
>
> —PROVERBS 4:23, NAS

> The hand of the diligent will rule, But the lazy man will be put to forced labor.
>
> —PROVERBS 12:24, NKJV

Diligence is a word that doesn't get a lot of press these days.

In some of the business bestsellers you might read about "due diligence," referring to the practice of considering all elements of a business plan in a systematic way.

Being diligent in *life* means paying attention to the details—those small and seemingly insignificant aspects of our daily routine that make all the difference between success and failure.

Diligence means applying yourself and doing your best—not other people's best and not in comparison to them. God wants you to be the best *you* can be, remembering that you are playing to an audience of One. Paul wrote, "Whatever you do, work at it with all your heart, as working for the Lord, not for men, since you know that you will receive an inheritance from the Lord as a reward. It's the Lord Christ you are serving" (Col. 3:23–24).

As a young seaman, former president Jimmy Carter served as an aide to Admiral Hyman Rickover, the father of the U.S. nuclear Navy, and was known to be a stickler for excellence. When reporting to his superior, Carter relayed his accomplishment of the task assigned, to which Admiral Rickover responded, "Did you do your best?"[3]

The young Carter dropped his head and walked away because he knew what that answer was. This taught him a lesson that he would never forget, and one he carried into the White House: always do your best.

Trustworthiness

> He who is faithful in what is least is faithful also in much.
>
> —LUKE 16:10, NKJV

In this passage, Jesus makes it clear that if you're not faithful in the little things in life, there's no use kidding yourself: you won't be faithful in the truly important things, either. The Greek word translated as *faithful* is rendered *trustworthy* in the NIV (see Luke 16:11). In other words, people can count on you. If you say you'll do it, they can bank on the fact that you will. Faithfulness is also listed in Galatians 5:22–23 as a beautiful fruit of God's Holy Spirit.

I once had an acquaintance with a somewhat careless attitude toward her belongings. "Oh, don't worry about the carpet," she would say. "I'll get a new one soon." That's the way it was with almost everything she had. She lived in the blissful confidence that she could eventually upgrade and replace everything. I didn't say anything at the time, but I couldn't help wondering, "Why should God provide you with something new when you don't take care of what He's already provided?"

Hard work

> All hard work brings a profit, but mere talk leads only to poverty.
>
> —PROVERBS 14:23

For many people work is a four-letter word. We can blame Adam for the need to work hard. Part of the consequences of the curse that entered the world through his disobedience was that man would make a living from the sweat of his brow. (See Genesis 3:17–19.) Notice that God cursed the ground and not Adam.

This negative view of hard work is a relatively new thing. Historically, because of Christianity's strong influence on Western culture, hard work was seen as a virtue and another vital way of worshiping God. People wanted to please the Master and took pride in a job well done. This was a direct outgrowth of a stewardship mentality: putting in an honest day's work for an honest wage.

Hard work alone, however, won't ensure prosperity. You can work hard at the wrong things and be farther behind than ever, or you can apply yourself to the right things and experience the blessing of God. What are these "right things"? Jesus said, "Do not labor for the food which perishes, but for the food which endures to everlasting life" (John 6:27, NKJV).

Trusting God as your source

> And my God will meet all your needs according to his glorious riches in Christ Jesus.
>
> —PHILIPPIANS 4:19

Trusting God as our ultimate source means that we cannot trust ourselves and our own human abilities to make our way. Seeing ourselves as the source is playing God—and a symptom of sinful pride. Acknowledging that all we have comes from the hand of a loving Father will help us see things correctly and understand that He is our only source.

Here in North America, the trend to move from the family farm into urban areas has separated most people from the land. It's not always easy to see the direct correlation between the food on our table and God's provision—not in the same way a farmer can when he raises the cow, slaughters the cow, and eats the cow. This makes it easy to look to our jobs as our source instead of seeing God as our provider.

I'm no fisherman and have very little desire to become one. I can think of other ways I'd rather enjoy my leisure hours. Years ago, however, a friend talked me into going salmon fishing with him. It was early in my marriage and money was tight, so the thought of a few succulent salmon steaks in the freezer had some appeal.

Our pessimistic guide on that little expedition reminded us that it was the wrong time of year and that the fish hadn't been biting for some time. But I had some help from on high. One of the seniors in our church had covenanted to pray that I would catch three fish: two for me and one for him. My friend, the experienced fisherman, came up totally empty that day, while I caught—you guessed it—three beautiful salmon. I was never so grateful to have food on the table as I was that day, because I saw the direct correlation between what was on my plate and the provision of God. My elderly friend was happy about it, too!

A life of gratitude

> Give thanks in all circumstances, for this is God's will for you in Christ Jesus.
>
> —1 THESSALONIANS 5:18

Does it ever bother you when people neglect or refuse to acknowledge an act of kindness? They act as if they *deserve* what they've received—that it's their "right" somehow.

I wonder if our lack of gratitude ever annoys God.

The life of a follower of Christ should be one marked by gratitude. As you leaf through the gospel accounts, there weren't very many things that caused Jesus to marvel, but Luke tells the story of one such case.

Ten men afflicted by the horrible disease of leprosy begged Jesus to heal them, and He granted their request. Jesus cleansed them all and instructed them to show themselves to the priest, be declared clean, and admitted back into the mainstream of society. One of them, seeing that his once-diseased skin was suddenly like that of a little child, returned and threw himself at the feet of Jesus to thank Him from the bottom of his heart. Jesus took note that ten men had been cleansed that day, but only one returned to give thanks. (See Luke 17:11–19.)

How often are you and I more like the ungrateful nine? How often do we stuff God's wondrous bounty into our pockets and hurry on our way without as much as a glance toward heaven? Acknowledging God as our source will have this positive benefit: We will be grateful because we see everything as coming from His hand.

No people in the history of the world have had as much materially as North Americans—or enjoyed it less. This carries over into the American church. As a general rule we are not a grateful people. Our love of material goods and the life of ease make us greedy, rather than grateful.

Andrew Carnegie, famous multi-millionaire and philanthropist from the last century, was asked "How much is enough?" Carnegie answered, "Just a little bit more."[4]

Cultivating a lifestyle of giving

> Heal the sick, raise the dead, cleanse those who have leprosy, drive out demons. Freely you have received, freely give.
> —MATTHEW 10:8

People who garden know that you must turn over the soil that has become caked and hardened over the winter. It usually takes a spade or shovel to break the ground, rendering it receptive to the new seeds. On farms a cultivator is a piece of equipment that does the very same thing, only on a larger scale. It loosens the soil so the planter can deposit the seeds into an environment that gives them the best chance of germinating and taking root.

Sowing seed is an act of giving. The seed must leave the hand of the sower. Once it does, the sower has very little control over the crop. He must trust the soil, the sun, the rain, and the goodness of God to cause the increase.

Like the gardener and the farmer, we too have a "hard soil" challenge. We must partner with the work of the Holy Spirit in our lives to break up the crusty ground that makes us resistant to good seeds and from producing good spiritual fruit in our lives.

Giving is one such fruit, and for most of us it doesn't come naturally. We must make a conscious choice to become givers.

Have you noticed that people who give tend to be the same people who receive? They understand the economics of the Kingdom of God: "Give, and it will be given to you" (Luke 6:38). But no farmer on the planet gets to harvest what hasn't been planted. A giving spirit is a characteristic of a child of God, in the same way that children resemble their parents and reflect their values. Our heavenly Father gives, and so should we. He gives because He loves, and so should we—without thought of return, or what's in it for us.

Who has ever said it better than Jesus?

Freely you have received, freely give.

—MATTHEW 10:8

CHAPTER 3

A CLOUD OF WITNESSES

*Therefore, since we are surrounded by such a great cloud of
witnesses, let us throw off everything that hinders.*

—HEBREWS 12:1

B LUE LIGHTS FLASHING, a police car rolls up to the scene of a
multiple-car traffic accident. Crunching broken glass under
his boot heels, the officer quickly surveys the scene to render
needed assistance.

Seeing that there are no injuries, the policeman nods at a
colleague who directs traffic around the wreck and promptly pulls
out a clipboard.

Why?

Because gaining information about an accident requires lots
of questions. Tracking down as many witnesses as possible, the
authorities will seek to view the incident from different angles and
perspectives—to get at what happened and why.

In a similar way, if we want to gain an accurate picture of what
the Bible says about giving, tithing in particular, we'll need to seek
out the best witnesses and ask good questions.

Witness #1: Abraham

Any discussion on the subject of tithing must begin with Abraham, rather than with Moses. Starting here is important, because some argue that tithing is part of the Law of Moses and, therefore, no longer required of Christians. According to their reasoning, Christians are inheritors of the New Covenant, and the Old Covenant given on Mount Sinai is no longer binding upon those saved by faith.

Those who adopt this argument usually talk a lot about "freedom in Christ" and how we are not under any obligation. From my experience, people who flee to this position usually use their freedom as an excuse not to tithe and often not to give to the Lord's work in any meaningful way at all.

However, tithing predates Moses!

Abraham, the father of those made righteous by faith (Rom. 4:17), tithed *before* the Mosaic Law ever came along. Abraham, therefore, set the pattern for the principle long before God revealed the Law to Moses on Mount Sinai.

Where did the concept of giving a tenth to God begin? All the way back in Genesis 14. When his nephew Lot was taken captive by an alliance of four kings, Abraham led his own private army and defeated the marauding rulers in a stunning, lightning-fast counterattack. He recaptured the possessions taken from his relative Lot in addition to other material wealth.

After such a crushing victory Abraham could certainly have claimed the spoils of war on the basis of his conquest. But he didn't. The biblical narrative records that Melchizedek, "priest of God Most High" (Gen. 14:18), greeted Abraham with bread and wine and blessed him. In return, Abraham "gave him a tenth of everything" (v. 20).

By these actions, Abraham acknowledged Melchizedek as a representative of God Most High, worthy of honor. He also declared that he would not profit or be made rich by the king of Sodom. (See Genesis 14:22–23.)

Did Abraham somehow sense the corrupting influence of earthly wealth, especially when gained through extraordinary circumstances? Did he understand by divine revelation the need to give a tenth? We aren't told. But what we do know is that he tithed to Melchizedek, king of Salem.

No one is really sure who Melchizedek was. The biblical record simply does not include enough information to make a positive identification. Some believe he was a pre-incarnate manifestation of Jesus or the Holy Spirit, a *theophany*, and conclude that Abraham tithed to God. People who hold this view base it on an interpretation of Hebrews 7:3, "Without father or mother, without genealogy, without beginning of days or end of life, like the Son of God he remains a priest forever." Intriguing as this thought might be, we can't be sure of it. What we can say, however, is that Abraham acknowledged Melchizedek as someone greater than himself, and he presented Melchizedek with a tenth.

Once again Scripture doesn't really tell us whether Abraham tithed on the spoils of battle or tithed on all that he owned in that encounter with the mysterious priest. We need to be careful not to go beyond what is written and stick with what we know for sure.

Abraham tithed.

The Bible doesn't say anything about an ongoing commitment to tithe on Abraham's part, but on this very significant occasion preserved for us through millennia of history, the patriarch gave one tenth to a representative of the Most High God.

Witness #2: Jacob

The next time we encounter the principle of tithing is in the story of Abraham's grandson, Jacob. Abraham's son Isaac had two sons: Esau and Jacob. Though fraternal twins, the boys couldn't have been more dissimilar. Esau was a rugged outdoorsman, while Jacob enjoyed the more civilized tent life. Esau lived for the moment with little or no thought for the future, while Jacob was a schemer, always on the look out for future gain.

On two separate occasions Jacob found a way to cheat Esau: by snatching away his older brother's birthright, and by outright stealing of the fatherly blessing intended for the firstborn son.

Enraged by these events, Esau vowed to kill his brother. To protect Jacob, Isaac and Rebekah sent their youngest son away to the land of his mother to escape his brother's wrath, find a wife, and rebuild his life. On the way, Jacob had the first of many encounters with God that would forever change his life.

At the place he would later name Bethel, or *House of God*, Jacob dreamed about a stairway stretching from the earth into heaven. The Lord Himself stood at the top and promised to bless the young fugitive. (See Genesis 28:10–15.) Early the next morning Jacob erected an altar to commemorate this supernatural event, vowing, "Of all that you give me I will give you a tenth" (Gen. 28:22).

That was a tremendous statement of faith from a man who truly possessed *nothing*. Jacob had fled from his home with nothing more than his staff in his hand and the clothes on his back. By faith he embraced the promise of God. Like his grandfather, Jacob acknowledged a power outside of himself, worthy of honor and homage. Before Jacob even had any material wealth, he purposed in his heart to honor God by tithing.

What is significant here? The example of Jacob comes in the form of a precedent and not a commandment. Jacob made the vow of his own volition. No law existed demanding he do this.

Where did he learn the principle of tithing? Did his father, Isaac, tithe? Did his grandfather, Abraham, pass on this principle directly to Jacob in the form of family history? We don't know for sure. What we do know is that these early patriarchs all shared the same faith in a personal God who had entered into a covenant relationship with them and had promised to bless them and provide for their needs.

Witness #3: Moses

Moses stands out in human history because of the massive influence Judaism and Christianity have exercised upon Western Civilization. The Mosaic Law received by Moses on Mount Sinai formed the basis of what was considered right and wrong and governed the spiritual and moral conduct of Israelite society.

The book of Leviticus outlines the Law in great detail and specifies what was required by the Israelites and the Levites in their worship of God: "A tithe of everything from the land, whether grain from the soil or fruit from the trees, belongs to the LORD; it is holy to the LORD" (Lev. 27:30). The Israelites were required to tithe on the produce of the land: the seed and fruit. This covers all that grows from the plant kingdom. Leviticus 27:32 adds, "The entire tithe of the herd and flock—every tenth animal that passes under the shepherd's rod—will be holy to the LORD." The tithe also extended to include the flocks and herds.

This wasn't a once-for-all tithe on an individual's herds, flocks, and stockpiled grain accumulated over the years. The tithe was to be ten percent of the *new* crop and the *additions* to the herds and the flocks.

Notice the Levites and priests weren't exempt. The Lord instructed Moses, "Speak to the Levites and say to them: 'When you receive from the Israelites the tithe I give you as your inheritance, you must present a tenth of that tithe as the Lord's offering'" (Num. 18:25–26).

In my life as a Christian I have been surprised and saddened to discover that some people in pastoral ministry who receive remuneration for their service to the church—roughly the modern equivalent of the priests and Levites—don't tithe or give offerings.

That's just wrong.

How can a person in vocational ministry expect others to have the faith and discipline to tithe when he does not, or feels he cannot, tithe? (See Leviticus 27:32–33.)

Deuteronomy 14:22–29 contains more specific details on the "hows" of tithing in the Mosaic Law. Here is a quick summary of this important passage:

We see the principle of setting aside a tenth each year of all that is added to a person in that year (the increase).

Because of the distance and logistics, it was permissible to change the substance of the tithes; in other words, people could convert produce and animals into silver, the equivalent of our cash.

God permitted the people to use some of the tithe money to buy a celebration meal, to be eaten in the Lord's presence. The purpose of this celebration meal was so that the person might *revere the Lord*—to think about God's provision and blessing over the year.

The Israelites were admonished not to forget the Levites, who were the vocational ministers of their day.

The tithe mentioned in this passage seems to be somewhat different; every third year, the tithe was to be stored in a local place to meet the physical needs of the Levites, aliens, fatherless, and widows. This provided a blessing for these people and served as a safeguard for the society.

Witness #4: Nehemiah

During the time of exile in Babylon, God raised up a dynamic leader and champion to restore His discouraged people. Nehemiah left the security of a high-level government job and the comfort of a palace in Persia to embrace the challenge of uniting a ragtag group of returnees dedicated to rebuilding Jerusalem.

Although the Israelites returned to their land and had lived there for almost a century, nothing much had been done for the city's infrastructure; the walls and gates of Jerusalem remained in ruin, leaving the people defenseless and at the mercy of their enemies. With God's help and with the commitment of the people to work, this remnant of a once-proud people succeeded in restoring Jerusalem. The book of Nehemiah chronicles the many things that had to be done to rebuild the community of God both physically and spiritually.

Once secure behind rebuilt city walls, however, the people forgot their commitment to God and His priests and Levites. Instead of being able to give themselves to the work of the ministry, the Levites found themselves working in the field to provide roofs over their heads and food on their tables. The failure on the part of the people to support God's house with tithes and offerings caused the spiritual climate of the restored community to languish. The ministry suffered when the people withheld their funds, as those "called" to vocational ministry had to seek other ways to provide for their needs.

Nehemiah, now the governor, rebuked the people for neglecting the "house of God" and set out to rectify the situation. (See Nehemiah 13:10–14.)

This same challenge confronts the present day people of God. Perhaps the contemporary church suffers because some of the *Levites*—those who should be devoting themselves to vocational ministry—are out laboring in the fields (the workplace), because the people of the church have misplaced their priorities as badly as the people in Nehemiah's day. A word needs to be said about being bi-vocational. From my perspective, most people who answer a call to recognized ministry are bi-vocational because the congregation they serve cannot support them. We do, however, see that a person might choose this, as in the case of the Apostle Paul. One could argue that he made this choice because he did not want to offend or burden the people.

Think about the pastors across our land who have to concern themselves with making the next rent check or simply purchasing a bag of groceries for their family. Does this pressure cripple those pastors and keep them from accomplishing their calling in the community? Does it rob them of the time and energy to think strategically and hear from God?

Of course it does.

Because we live in a material world, the work of God here on earth cannot be carried on without the material support of God's people. Giving tithes and offerings, then and now, is God's method for supporting His ministry and His ministers. God set something in motion that required faith and commitment on the part of His people to partner with Him. Like the Levites, those called to vocational ministry depend upon the tithes and offerings of God's people to meet their needs so that they can devote themselves to serving.

Witness #5: Haggai

When Jerusalem fell to Babylonian invaders in 586 B.C., many of the inhabitants who weren't slain were marched off into exile in faraway Babylon. True to His word, God heard the prayers of His people, and in 538 B.C. King Cyrus of Persia issued a decree allowing the Jews to return to their ancestral home and rebuild the city.

During the seventy years of exile the people of God experienced a massive change in perspective. Living among the affluent Babylonians, they began to adopt a much more secular approach to life. Those who made their way back to Jerusalem began to rebuild the temple, but soon lost interest as they became caught up in other life pursuits.

After more than a decade had passed, the prophet Haggai rebuked the people because they were living in paneled houses while the temple, the symbol of religious and community life, remained in ruins. Because the people weren't putting God first and honoring Him with their tithes and offerings, they were, in effect, putting their money in purses with holes: in places where their material wealth would slip through their fingers. (See Haggai 1:3–9.)

Is there anything wrong with living in a nicely paneled house? At first reading this could appear to be attack on "having nice things." Not so. That wasn't the message of the prophet. It wasn't the paneled houses that were the problem; it was neglect of God's house. As with the Jews in Haggai's time, God's people still face the strong temptation to build their personal wealth and security while His "house" languishes.

Unless we choose otherwise, we will build our own "houses" and feather our own nests instead of putting the kingdom of God first. Money gravitates toward *paneled houses*—things that make life here on earth more comfortable and easier, and not things that are eternal.

Witness #6: Malachi

Because the book of Malachi has been so frequently quoted in support of tithing, it deserves its own chapter. (See Chapter 4.)

Witness #7: Jesus

Historically the church has included tithing as part of Jesus' commandments to His church. Is that legitimate? Without qualification we can say Jesus endorsed liberal giving. "Give," He said, "and it will be given to you" (Luke 6:38).

Giving is to be part of the character and nature of the Christian because it's the character and nature of God. God is love, and love is both giving and sacrificial. Bearing this out, Jesus taught and modeled a life of giving.

Genesis 1:26 tells us that God created man in His image, in His likeness. Being created in His image means that we are spiritual beings, created to reflect His glory. Just as a human father passes on DNA, those born of God receive His spiritual DNA. One of the characteristics of our Father in heaven is that He is giving. If we are to resemble Him, then we should be givers, too.

In Luke 21:1–4, Jesus drives home the motivation for giving. Jesus and His disciples watched from the sidelines as different people put their gifts into the temple treasury. He saw the rich give lavishly, but what really caught His attention was a poor widow who dropped two very small coins in the offering.

Never one to miss a teaching moment, Jesus commented on the two different types of gifts and the two different types of givers.

The rich gave out of their abundance, while the poor widow gave all she had.

As lavish and extravagant as their gifts might have seemed to everyone else, the rich could pour enormous amounts of cash into the kettle (silver and gold make a lot of noise) and really not feel any financial pinch. The widow, however, took a giant step of faith, deliberately choosing to give God everything she owned with nothing held back.

And that was a sacrifice that drew the attention of God's Son.

The emphasis of the story is the motive of giving, not the amount.

Jesus wasn't advocating that everyone sell everything and put it in the offering. What He was doing, however, was turning the spotlight on the human heart. It comes back to where your treasure truly lies. (See Matthew 6:21.)

Jesus did specifically address the issue of tithing on at least two occasions: Matthew 22:21 and 23:23. In these two pointed exchanges with the Pharisees and the Sadducees, the religious establishment of the day, Jesus endorsed the principle of tithing.

Now not all the Pharisees were bad people. In fact, the New Testament records several instances where members of that strict religious order followed Jesus, Nicodemus, and Joseph of Arimathea. The problem with a sizeable majority of the Pharisees, however, was their external adherence to the letter of the Law of Moses, while being devoid internally of the character and nature of the God they claimed to serve. (See Matthew 23:27.) Jesus said of them, "These people honor me with their lips, but their hearts are far from me" (Matt. 15:8).

The context of Matthew 22:21 deserves a closer look. One of the scribes came to Jesus looking to trap Him into saying something that was either treasonous to Rome, the world power that occupied Judea, or a betrayal of the Messianic aspirations of the Jews, who were looking for a military and political leader to help them overthrow the hated Romans.

"Master," the scribe said, "is it lawful to pay taxes to Caesar?" His desire to maneuver Jesus into a corner went for naught. Jesus calmly asked him to produce a coin of the realm and said, "Give to Caesar what is Caesar's; and to God what is God's" (Matt. 22:21). Those trying to trap Jesus went away amazed.

There are at least two lessons here: (1) A follower of Jesus has a responsibility to give to the civil government what is required, and (2) A person who desires to please God has a responsibility to give to God what belongs to Him.

Jesus did not hedge when dealing with *Caesar*—human government.

Jesus was equally clear about giving God what was His due. This included giving monetarily, but involved so much more. Everything we have belongs to the God who, at great price, gave us life and bought us back from slavery and death.

In Matthew 23:23 Jesus specifically endorsed the principle of tithing. "Woe to you, teachers of the law and Pharisees, you hypocrites! You give a tenth of your spices—mint, dill and cummin. But you have neglected the more important matters of the law— justice, mercy and faithfulness. You should have practiced the latter, without neglecting the former."

This verse actually applies to all aspects of our Christian life. We see that God's concern is not for our money as an end in itself. We need to focus on the transformation He desires to work in our lives. He desires justice, mercy, and faithfulness. Some limit what God requires to simply exhibiting such character qualities. But if we finish the verse we see that Jesus also said, "You should have practiced [done] the latter without neglecting the former."

In other words, you shouldn't neglect your tithe.

In His Sermon on the Mount Jesus clearly articulated the need to go beyond outward adherence to a set of external rules, proclaiming, to all who would hear, the new ethics of the Kingdom of God. Jesus came to fulfill the Law of Moses, not to abolish it. (See Matthew 5:17–18.)

In addressing how a kingdom man or woman should act, Jesus called on His followers to lay aside worries over the necessities of life, trusting instead in a loving Father's provision. (See Matthew 6:25–33.)

As we follow Him, He will provide. That's His promise.

Witness #8: Paul

The church age opened with the community of believers giving liberally. The first chapters of Acts record many examples of generosity and sacrifice. People like Barnabas set a dramatic example of how individuals gave to the cause of advancing the gospel. (See Acts 4:36–37.)

This generous spirit wasn't limited to the believers in Jerusalem. Through the letters of Paul we read of other local churches that gave beyond their human ability. In his farewell speech to the elders of Ephesus, Paul quotes what must have been a well-known statement of Jesus in Acts 20:35, "Remembering the words the Lord Jesus himself said: 'It is more blessed to give than to receive.'"

The apostle Paul stands as a spiritual giant of our faith, planting churches throughout the Mediterranean basin and authoring almost half of the New Testament books. Born Saul of Tarsus, Paul grew up in a major trading center in the Roman Empire and attended the "University of Jerusalem," sitting at the feet of the noted teacher Gamaliel. His familiarity with both the Jewish and Gentile worlds uniquely qualified him to help the fledgling churches under his apostolic care to apply the teachings of Jesus to their circumstances.

Paul not only quoted Jesus, but also had much to say on the whole subject of money and honoring God with finances. Modeling servanthood, the apostle lived what he taught. He could have set himself up as a "king" in the churches he started. Instead he worked tirelessly to provide for his own physical needs by working in his trade. Having a trade was required for those serious about their studies of the Law. (As an aside, the term *tentmaking* is often used of the bi-vocational pastor in contemporary church circles; that is: a person who works a secular job so that he can fulfill his true call to be in church leadership.) He didn't want to give anyone occasion to accuse him of taking advantage of his position. (See 2 Thessalonians 3:7–10.)

Even though Paul worked hard to support himself in his ministry, he also took pains to underline the importance of supporting the work of the kingdom in a material way. "Those who preach the gospel," he declared, "should receive their living from the gospel" (1 Cor. 9:14).

Paul could speak to this issue with a strong voice, because he had learned the secret of being content in his circumstances, whether in plenty or in want. (See Philippians 4:11–12.) During the times that he had an abundance of physical and material resources, "being comfortable" didn't deter him from his mission or cause him to lose focus. Conversely, when resources were scarce he didn't complain, but continued to be faithful in his service to the Lord and to the churches.

Paul taught the emerging church a great deal about finances, making reference to money throughout his letters. In Romans 12:8 he refers to giving as a spiritual gift, urging those who contribute to the Lord's work to do so generously.

At the close of his first letter to the Corinthians, Paul gives specific instructions to the church to set aside money for the saints in Judea, who were suffering through a famine. Paul wanted the disciples to think beyond themselves.

The first two verses from 1 Corinthians 16 teach that regular and proportionate giving was to be the practice and pattern of this early church.

> Now about the collection for God's people: Do what I told the Galatian churches to do. On the first day of every week, each one of you should set aside a sum of money in keeping with his income, saving it up, so that when I come no collections will have to be made.

Note that the collection took place on Sunday, the "first day of every week." "Each one" refers to all who considered themselves a part of the community of believers there in Corinth. To "set aside" implies action and conscious choice. "In keeping with his income" speaks of giving in proportion to what a person has earned.

The Living Bible contains this wonderful paraphrase of verse two: "The amount depends on how much the Lord has helped you earn."

This captures the idea that the person gives in proportion to how God has blessed.

In his second letter to the Corinthians, Paul writes this instruction:

> Each man should give what he has decided in his heart to give, not reluctantly or under compulsion, for God loves a cheerful giver. And God is able to make all grace abound to you, so that in all things at all times, having all that you need, you will abound in every good work.
>
> —2 Corinthians 9:7–8

What are the principles in this passage?

- ♪ Giving must come from the heart.

- ♪ Giving is a decision, not an emotion.

- ♪ Giving is to be done freely and not out of obligation.

- ♪ As we give, God gives back to us.

- ♪ He blesses us so that we may "abound in every good work." In other words, God blesses so we can bless others. Giving releases abundance.

Paul also praised other churches that provided a good example. The apostle commended the church in Philippi for their "partnership in the Gospel" (Phil. 1:5). In 2 Corinthians 8:4 we read how this church gave above and beyond their ability, and desired to have the "privilege of sharing in this service to the saints." Paul uses their example to exhort the Corinthians to "excel in this grace of giving" (v. 7).

As a proud spiritual father, Paul wrote the Philippians a heartfelt blessing born of deep conviction, "And my God will meet all your needs according to his glorious riches in Christ Jesus" (Phil. 4:19).

Paul mentored individuals as well as churches, becoming a spiritual father to several young disciples. Writing to Timothy, one of his most promising young protégés, Paul gave very specific advice on how to approach the touchy subject of a believer and his money:

> Command those who are rich in this present world not to be arrogant nor to put their hope in wealth, which is so

uncertain, but to put their hope in God, who richly provides us with everything for our enjoyment. Command them to do good, to be rich in good deeds, and to be generous and willing to share.

—1 Timothy 6:17–18

People with material wealth, Paul told his young charge, are to be commanded not to put their trust in earthly possessions. Why do people possess things in the first place?

So that they can be a blessing to others.

CHAPTER 4

A MESSAGE FROM MALACHI

Bring your full tithe to the Temple treasury so there will be ample provisions in my Temple. Test me in this and see if I don't open up heaven itself to you and pour out blessings beyond your wildest dreams.

—MALACHI 3:10, THE MESSAGE

MALACHI'S CENTRAL MESSAGE is about as simple as it gets.

Put God first.

In a deeply heartfelt prophecy, Malachi called on the covenant community of the Jews to return God to His rightful place in their society and in their hearts.

As an example of the apathy and cynicism that had poisoned the nation's religious life, he pointed to the practice of many who were presenting blighted and blemished sacrifices to God: offering blind, crippled, and diseased animals instead of their best, as called for in the Law.

What they were doing really didn't even fall under the category of "sacrifice." Giving up something you can't use or don't need isn't a sacrifice—it's a sham.

Malachi challenges them with the rhetorical question, "Try offering them to your governor! Would he be pleased with you? Would he accept you?" (Mal. 1:8). It shouldn't amaze me, but somehow it always does: it's as though we think what's not good enough for people is somehow still good enough for God.

Malachi calls for a change of thinking and behavior on the part of God's people. And as it happens so often in the books of the prophets, along with the challenge and the warning comes a wonderful promise.

> "Will a man rob God? Yet you rob me. "But you ask, 'How do we rob you?' In tithes and offerings. You are under a curse—the whole nation of you—because you are robbing me. Bring the whole tithe into the storehouse, that there may be food in my house. Test me in this," says the Lord Almighty, "and see if I will not throw open the floodgates of heaven and pour out so much blessing that you will not have room enough for it."
> —MALACHI 3:8–10

Let's take a closer look at each phrase of this remarkable passage.

"Will a Man Rob God?"

Will a man rob God? Yet you rob me (v. 8).

Have you ever been accused of stealing something? It's pretty strong stuff, accusing people of theft! To rob is to take or withhold something that belongs to someone else. But how could a puny human being rob or steal from the God of the universe, the All-sufficient One who owns everything? This seems inconceivable and yet God Himself is the one who reports the theft in this passage.

The simple fact is that if they could rob God, then we can, too.

How do we do that? The same way they did. By withholding what is rightfully His. This can be either a passive behavior or a conscious choice. We passively rob God by putting Him out of our thoughts, out of our reckoning, out of our budgets, out of our daily lives. We actively and specifically rob God when we make a conscious decision not to honor Him or acknowledge His ownership by presenting Him with our tithes and offerings.

For the Old Testament believer, giving tithes and offerings was a command. For the New Testament believer, it's a principle. In the end, however, it really amounts to the same thing: acknowledging God's ownership of all He has entrusted into our care.

Notice that Malachi mentioned both tithes and offerings in his indictment. An offering, as understood in the Old Testament, was anything given over and above the tithe. An offering was an amount—any amount—freely offered beyond any requirement.

Let me be very clear here. God doesn't want us to give our tithes and offerings out of some misplaced sense of duty or fear of "robbing Him." He doesn't want us to give because we're terrified of the consequences if we don't. What delights His heart is when His children give out of a heart of love and an understanding of true worship.

True worship is always about heart, and heart is all about love, not fear.

Obedience to God certainly does bring blessing, but we can't earn God's love or favor by our actions, or "works of righteousness." (See Titus 3:5, KJV.)

Once we have accepted the free gift of salvation, we're not required to "do" anything more. We can't buy our way into heaven. We accept what Jesus did for us on the cross by faith, and faith alone.

Having said and reaffirmed those precious truths, now that we have accepted Jesus as Savior, we want to live our lives in a way that pleases Him. Honoring God, which includes our finances, opens the door for God to pour out His blessing. Our obedience does have an undeniable impact on our spiritual fruitfulness, which has a direct bearing on the rewards we will enjoy through all eternity.

"You are Under a Curse"

> You are under a curse—the whole nation of you—because you are robbing me (v. 9).

People in positions of authority within the church have used this verse as a weapon to bludgeon their parishioners. Speakers conjure up images of a spiteful, or even wrathful, God who sits on the edge of heaven, lightning bolts in hand, waiting for any excuse to lash out against man, His poor, hapless creation. God gets portrayed as a malevolent Supreme Being who actively curses and punishes those who refuse to toe His line.

It's a lie right out of the pit.

Nothing could be further from the truth.

God desires to bless His children.

What then, do we do with Malachi 3:9, which states quite emphatically that those who rob God are under a curse? And how do we apply this to real life in a way that brings encouragement, rather than fear and condemnation?

This might take just a little explanation.

We talk about both blessing and cursing, but do we understand these concepts in today's world? I thought I had this all figured out until I was challenged (in a good way) with the question, "But Pastor Tom...doesn't God curse people?"

This forced me to go back to my Bible (always a good thing) to take a closer look at this business of curses. A curse is when evil or harm comes to someone as a result of their failure to do something or their violation of a divine prohibition. When you curse someone you invoke God's wrath or invite evil into their lives. This type of cursing is not consistent with the good God portrayed in the Bible. God does not wish or desire evil to happen to anyone. Nor does He inflict evil upon people.

I see blessing or cursing as the natural consequence of obedience or disobedience. Obedience brings blessing. Disobedience brings cursing. (See Deuteronomy 11:27–27.) You are "cursed" when you aren't living under the complete blessing of God. God cannot bless disobedience. When we are outside of God's obedience and favor, the curse is self-fulfilling; we see the consequences of sin coming home to roost in the lives of people who make bad choices. This is very different matter from a vengeful God taking out His anger and frustration on people He considers disobedient.

We can't, however, get away from the reality that when sin entered the world it brought with it a curse. (See Genesis 3.)

And the curse was unimaginably terrible and far-reaching.

Physical death came as a result, just as God had warned Adam and Eve. So did the need to earn a living by the sweat of our brow and pain in childbirth. All sickness, pain, suffering, and sorrow rolled across our world on the same dark tide. As bad as all that may have been, the worst result by far was a broken relationship with God.

But God had a remedy in mind even for that, and announced it in Genesis 3:15 before He spoke of the consequences of man's sin. The only remedy would be God's interjecting Himself into the fatally flawed world in the person of Jesus, who came to redeem and restore that relationship between creature and Creator through His death on the cross. The blood of Jesus broke the power of Eden's curse.

The opposite of cursing is blessing. To bless someone or to speak a blessing is the action of declaring or invoking God's favor—inviting His goodness into someone's life. Blessing reflects the true image of the God of love who desires the very best for all mankind.

For the ancient Hebrew, words had great power. Once a blessing was given, the words took on a life of their own. Receiving the father's blessing was worth the risk—the father's displeasure, or even death. (See Genesis 27.)

Keep in perspective that this curse to which Malachi refers has nothing to do with our standing with God. We are saved by faith and not by works. (See Ephesians 2:8–9.) Whether we tithe or not has nothing to do with God's gift of eternal life and the promise of heaven. Our position with God is based wholly and solely upon our acceptance of Jesus' work on the cross.

Some have adopted a theology of "generational" curses, and see these as the explanation for all that is bad in their lives. Digging into their family histories, they look for reasons why they're not enjoying the fullness of God's favor and bounty.

The truth is: generational "curses" are simply a reflection of generational patterns of sin—sons and daughters repeating the sins of fathers and mothers. Christ came to proclaim liberty and freedom for the captives and those bound by sin. This includes changing behavioral and thought patterns that bind people up and keep them from experiencing the fullness of God's generosity and kindness.

Wrong thinking about finances is an example of the kind of negative generational patterns that keep many people from walking in the new things God has in store. Jesus has set us free from the curse of sin and from the power of generational curses. When we discover where we appear to be bound, we need to break the curse's hold over us.

I personally believe that we are bound to the degree that we believe we are bound. This gets communicated in seemingly simple phrases like, "Well, Granddad had a bad temper, and I guess I just inherited it from him."

Jesus promises to change us into His likeness. It's a process that unfolds in our lives as we cooperate with the daily transforming work of God's Holy Spirit in the very core of our lives. (See 2 Corinthians 5:17.)

While we need to be aware of past patterns and family strongholds, God wants us to look to our future, and not the past. Jerry Cook says it like this, "God comes to us from our future and not our past."

A few weeks ago I was out walking with one of the guys in our church. He had experienced a great deal of brokenness in his life, growing up in an unbelievably dysfunctional family. He shared with me how God had set him free from a life of addictions and wrong thinking. But he was also wondering when he could begin to expect God's blessings to become evident in his life as a result of right living. Specifically, he wanted to see some financial blessings.

After he finished I tried to explain what God had been showing me about wise choices in life and the tangible blessings that follow. The truth is: people may not see direct financial results growing out of a life of obedience to God. But their children might. When boys and girls grow up in a stable family, free from the struggle of dysfunction and crippling patterns of sin, they are able to make good choices not available to their parents.

I went on to talk to him about my own family. All four of my grandparents made adult decisions for Christ. Only one of them graduated from high school. Their children—my parents—went on to do well, and now my brother and I both have university educations that have opened doors for us that our grandparents could only dream about.

So what is this curse Malachi is talking about? Simply put, the curse is not living under God's blessing. It is the heart of God to bless His children. By not honoring Him with our tithes and offerings, we take ourselves out of a place where God can fill our lives with His goodness and where He can work supernaturally on our behalf to supply our material needs.

Message for "the Whole Nation"

You are under a curse—the whole nation of you (v. 9).

Malachi writes that his message was for everyone, not just a select few.

This also means you and me, today. Right now.

Honoring God with tithes and offerings was to be practiced by the whole covenant community. In our humanness we sometimes like to think that certain laws and directives (such as speed limits) are for "someone else."

When it comes to tithes and offerings to support the work of the Lord, there is no "someone else." God's standards and expectations apply to every one of His redeemed children.

"Bring"

Bring the whole tithe into the storehouse (v. 10).

The word "bring" conveys the idea of conscious choice and action. It also carries with it the idea of making a presentation. When we give gifts at Christmas time or on special occasions, we wrap them up and hand-deliver them, in person. It's a loving, personal act.

The verb "bring" assumes that a person is a part of the church community and has a spiritual home where tithes and offerings can be presented. You can make that presentation in a variety of ways. Some churches have an offering box. Others pass the plate. In some fellowships bringing tithes and offerings means physically taking them to the front of the church as an act of worship.

The methods may vary, but the principle remains constant: making a conscious choice to give to God in honor of His provision.

What is "the Whole"?

Bring the *whole* tithe into the storehouse (v. 10).

So what constitutes "the whole"? Your gross income is your whole income before anything has been deducted. Your net income is *take home pay*—what you have left after subtracting things like payroll deductions, taxes, and pension plan contributions.

In making this determination of the whole, be careful of rationalization. Every one of us has a tendency to convince ourselves that something is "okay" even when we know deep down inside that it really isn't.

Some people, for instance, "tithe" after deducting their rent or mortgage. They rationalize by saying, "I never see it, so it's not really mine." Once a person goes down that road, however, where does it end? Do we tithe after paying the utilities? After buying the groceries? After making the car payment? Bringing a tithe of *the whole*—our gross salary—objectifies the process, and protects us from becoming subjective or arbitrary in giving to God.

Many Christians today base their giving upon "what they feel led to bring," with little or no thought to the principles and boundaries laid out in the Bible. They live on the basis of subjective feelings and not upon the principles of the Kingdom of God. These biblical principles provide an external safety rail that keeps us from careening off the road and into the ditch.

What is "the Storehouse"?

Bring the whole tithe into the *storehouse* (v. 10).

The people in Malachi's day had no difficulty understanding where and what the "storehouse" was. They knew very well the prophet was talking about God's temple.

But that was then. What is the storehouse for us today? Where does my tithe belong?

To answer this question let's examine the concept of *dynamic equivalents*, one of the universal and time-honored principles of hermeneutics—how we interpret the Bible. This principle speaks of how something translates from one culture and time to another. In the process, the two basic questions of hermeneutics surface: (1) "What did it mean to the original hearer?" and (2) "What does it mean for me today?"

What, then, is the dynamic equivalent of the storehouse for us today? Is it the local church or some other ministry?

Let's start with what the storehouse was for the original hearers. God's temple in Jerusalem was a physical building at a specific location. First Kings 8 records that God, whom the highest heavens can't contain, chose Jerusalem as the location for His temple on earth. He designated the temple as the place where His people would worship Him by offering sacrifices and by bringing their tithes and offerings. In fact, the temple complex had literal storerooms as a part of its design.

The Bible records that more than one tithe existed in ancient Israel: (1) what they brought to God to make sure there was food in the temple, and (2) one for the king, which is equivalent to our taxes. The tithe referred to in Malachi is the first type, and was given to make sure there were material resources in the temple. The purpose of this tithe was to meet the needs of the priests and Levites who ministered before the Lord, as well as the poor and needy; that is to say, they made sure there was food in the temple.

So the storehouse was just that; it was a physical location where people brought a tithe of their increase and presented offerings. The temple was a resource center to meet both spiritual and physical needs.

The dynamic (contemporary) equivalent of the storehouse mentioned in Malachi would be the local church—not the building, but all that encompasses our understanding of church. People come together at a central location to create a resource center where spiritual and physical needs can be met.

Malachi echoed Moses' command to the people, "But take your consecrated things and whatever you have vowed to give, and go to the place the LORD will choose" (Deut. 12:26). This shows us that we must be careful not to make an arbitrary decision about where we present our tithes.

There are advantages to tithing to a local church in this way. To begin with, you can observe firsthand how those tithes are being used. You will know whether things are out of balance or if there is a misuse of funds. Healthy leaders and healthy churches will encourage you to ask questions about their use of monies, and are willing to be accountable. I wouldn't attend any church where I couldn't trust the leadership with my tithes and offerings.

"Food in My House"

> Bring the whole tithe into the storehouse, that there may be food in my house (v. 10).

The tithes and offerings are collected and used wisely to ensure that there is "food" in the spiritual storehouse. In the Old Testament, the tithes supported the priests and Levites; in contemporary times, the tithes support vocational ministers who are able to devote their focus to the work of serving God's people.

In a very real sense people "eat of their tithes" each time the church gathers publicly and they receive spiritual food from the ministry and teaching. In Deuteronomy 12:5–7, Moses spoke about that future day when the Israelites would approach the place of God's choosing:

> But you are to seek the place the LORD your God will choose from among all your tribes to put his Name there for his dwelling. To that place you must go; there bring your burnt offerings and sacrifices, your tithes and special gifts, what you have vowed to give and your freewill offerings, and the firstborn of your herds and flocks. There, in the presence of the LORD your God, you and your families shall eat and shall rejoice in everything you have put your hand to, because the LORD your God has blessed you.

Deuteronomy 12 contains some other important points:

§   God is the one who has chosen the place where the tithe is to be brought.

- The ancient Israelites who traveled from a distance were permitted to eat and partake of their tithes and offerings while in the place where God had chosen.

- It would have been impossible to consume all of the tithes and offerings, so the excess was stored at the central location.

What about the parachurch?

Wait a minute. We need to take an important detour here. If my tithe belongs to the local church, what about the parachurch organizations and other ministries that aren't a part of my local church?

The Greek word *para* means, "to come along side," so a *parachurch* organization is one that "walks alongside of the church."

Frankly, I struggle with this.

The church is the church.

What these organizations do is a very real part of the mission of the church. Parachurch organizations don't support the church, but are genuine expressions of the church.

The emergence of parachurch organizations and television ministries, however, complicates the discussion about the "storehouse." Many valid ministries of this nature exist. And, like all ministries, they need help and support.

My concern is that such ministries siphon off resources that belong to the local assembly.

What about the need for the touch of a local pastor, someone whom you know and who knows you? My first pastorate was in a tiny community on Vancouver Island in the province of British Columbia. The church was small and, like most churches big or small, we struggled financially. Yes, God always supplied our needs. But the lack of financial support from the church greatly limited ministry in that place.

As I talked with people who considered themselves to be committed to me and the local church there, I discovered that hundreds, if not thousands of dollars—a lot of money in 1980— were being sent to TV and worldwide ministries. And yet when a problem arose, who did they call? It wasn't some 800 number on the bottom of the TV screen. They called me. Why? Because I was the person who was local and who they considered to be their pastor.

Isn't the laborer "worthy of his hire"? (See Luke 10:7, KJV.) Shouldn't people make sure that the local pastor receives adequate remuneration to carry on the ministry in their community?

I realize that for many people with physical conditions that prevent attendance at a local fellowship, the "church of the airwaves" is the only place they receive ministry in the course of the week. If we accept that the whole tithe belongs to the church where a person attends and is fed, then a person who is shut in and can't get out to a local church should give to a television ministry. That is, in fact, their "storehouse."

Although we are to bring our tithes to our spiritual home where we belong and are being fed spiritually, our offerings can go wherever we feel led to give them. Where we give our offerings should be in keeping with our philosophy of ministry, our spiritual values, and our priorities. We should give in an intentional manner—not out of crisis or emotional appeals.

"Test Me in This"

"Test me in this," says the LORD Almighty, "and see if I will not throw open the floodgates of heaven" (v. 10).

God was saying to His people, "Prove My word true. Trust Me. Step out in faith and watch Me provide for your needs."

When God says, "Test Me," it has nothing to do with expecting Him to bail us out of the consequences of our own rash or foolish choices or actions.

Just because we have faith in God, tithe, and give offerings doesn't mean that we are free to "test" the Lord by misapplying Malachi 3:8–10. I have known some people who have believed they could survive a blind and foolish leap from a pinnacle of financial peril that they reached all on their own. They continued to run the red lights that should have kept them from making serious mistakes, assuming themselves covered or untouchable because of a misunderstanding of the phrase, "Test Me in this."

Don't be foolish. Trust God and be obedient to honor Him in all ways, including with your finances. Then, and only then, can you claim the promise of Malachi 3:8–10.

We're really talking about here is how a faithful God will meet our legitimate needs: bread on the table, clothes on our body, a roof over our heads. This, of course, assumes that a person knows the difference between a want and a need. What's more, to recognize this opening of the heavenly realm, we need to look beyond what we can see with our natural eyes.

In all my years as a Christian, I have yet to see any physical windows open from the sky to pour out financial blessing. Sometimes I get the feeling that people expect this to happen literally, in the same way that a slot machine pays off when someone hits the jackpot.

The promise to "open the windows of heaven" by no means guarantees material wealth and prosperity. Do new SUVs fall from the windows of heaven? Speedboats? Caribbean cruises? Designer clothing?

But don't mistake me here. I certainly have seen God open the windows of heaven—times beyond number.

Blessing, including financial blessing, isn't always *in kind*. When you give in dollars you may not receive a return in dollars. God is much more creative than that! Sometimes the blessing and miracle of provision will be in another form. God's "return" for faithful giving may come in the form of an idea that will revolutionize your business. It may take place in a very miraculous, but subtle, way where money goes farther than it physically or logically should. In fact, we may never see some of the many ways God has opened His windows of blessing and provided for us until we are in heaven.

I've noticed something else about celestial windows being opened. The people who give are usually the very ones who receive. A giving person becomes a conduit through which God can pour His blessing upon others. Remember, God uses people to do His will here on earth. This is the fulfillment of Proverbs 11:25 that says, "The generous man will be prosperous, And he who waters will himself be watered" (NAS).

The geography of the Middle East provides a pointed illustration of what happens when people become a channel of God's blessing, and when they don't. The map shows two large bodies of water on the border between Israel and Jordan: the Sea of Galilee and the Dead Sea. One teems with life, the Sea of Galilee. The other, the Dead Sea, choked with mineral salinity, kills any fish within minutes that unfortunately makes its way into its waters.

What's the major difference between these two bodies of water? The Sea of Galilee has an inflow and an outflow that allows it to be continually renewed. The Dead Sea has no outflow. It is not renewed, but grows saltier with the passage of time. And that makes it "Dead."

In a similar way our giving provides an outflow for our lives that creates a place for new things to enter. Giving provides for refreshing and renewal.

Honoring the principle of tithing requires faith. It is putting our faith into action that unlocks and opens the "windows of heaven." Faith releases the supernatural supply of God. One reason people don't give is fear that there won't be enough to meet their needs. Fear, however, is the opposite of faith. Faith makes it possible for God to bless. Fear causes people to hoard and clogs the pipeline of blessing.

"I Will Rebuke the Devourer"

> And I will rebuke the devourer for your sakes, and he shall
> not destroy the fruits of your ground.
> —MALACHI 3:11, KJV

Most Christians assume the devourer in this passage is the devil. So when bad things happen that erode their financial position, the devil gets the blame. This may be true, but the devil isn't responsible for all the difficulties and hardships that come our way.

Life can devour our resources. Energy costs can skyrocket without warning, as they did during the 1973 oil embargo, and again in 2006. Unexpected expenses occur. Surprise repairs or catastrophic illness gobble up and devour our financial resources. Inflation eats away at our buying power and a dollar just doesn't go as far as it used to.

Even tithing Christians may have to make adjustments in their standard of living. It's not an inalienable right that we will enjoy an ever-increasing level of financial prosperity and comfort. Can we trust that God will make ends meet, even in a seemingly hostile economy? The answer is straightforward. Either the principles of

God work, or they don't, regardless of the external circumstances beyond our control.

The economy of God's kingdom is based upon His eternal principles and truths; it's not tied to the economy of this world. If the spiritual dynamics of good stewardship and God's provision can only work in a super-heated North American economy, we are really in trouble.

Many things can and will devour our financial reserves, and yet Malachi communicates God's promise to rebuke this erosion of precious resources. What are some ways that God will "rebuke the devourer"? One way that God does this is by making what we have last longer and go farther. For instance, we will run across sales where we can make great savings at the very time we need something—like a new coat or a set of tires for the car.

The list is endless, but you won't see how God provides in this way unless you're looking. When you see good things happen, acknowledge God's provision. Don't miss God's hand of blessing by assigning something good to blind chance or dumb luck. How often do you hear people say, "God hasn't done anything for me"? Well, He probably has done a great deal for them. They just don't acknowledge it, or they haven't really had their eyes open to see it.

An orderly life governed by godly principles greatly reduces the places where a person can be robbed—where the enemy of our soul gains a foothold through wrong thinking or practice that gives him access to steal from us what God desires to give. A person who lives by godly principles will make sound financial decisions based upon stewardship, instead of living day to day with little thought to the consequences of their choices. People who see themselves as stewards take better care of their bodies. Once again the list is endless: stewardship impacts everything in our lives.

"Then All the Nations Will Call You Blessed"

"Then all the nations will call you blessed, for yours will be a delightful land," says the LORD Almighty (v. 12).

The "nations" referred to here were the peoples who lived in the areas around Israel. In our context, the dynamic equivalents of "the nations" are the non-Christians in our families and neighborhoods. Our faith in God's provision and well-ordered lives are meant to show the glory of God to a world that needs enlightenment, direction, and hope.

The Bible reveals the unfolding plan God had for Israel. God chose the descendants of Abraham to be a light to the nations: a people who would reflect the goodness and care of a loving God. Tragically, the Israelites failed to grasp this concept. Lest we become too judgmental, however, I'm not sure that the contemporary church, also formed by a covenant people, has performed much better. God intended His redeemed ones to be examples, living orderly, joyous lives.

What does being blessed look like? The wealth and affluence of the present day North American church has permitted some to put their own spin on the theology of prosperity and God's blessing. Some teach that God's blessing and material wealth go hand in hand. This theology has been dubbed the "Prosperity Gospel." Some endorse this "gospel" to such an extent that they measure people's spirituality—and even their relationship with God—by how much they have materially in this life.

The message of the Gospel, however, was never about material blessings, but rather about the spiritual riches Jesus came to bestow upon all who would trust in Him. The proof of our acceptance by God is the price paid upon the cross, not by how much we paid for our watch.

The apostle John defined prosperity when he wrote: "Beloved, I pray that in all respects you may prosper and be in good health, just as your soul prospers" (3 John 2, NAS). True prosperity is to be measured by the condition of our spiritual lives. If our spiritual lives are in order, this will point the rest of our lives in the right direction.

Any theology we adopt must include the understanding that Christians, even godly, obedient ones, sometimes suffer hardship and don't always have their wants satisfied. By adopting a more balanced theology of prosperity, we are in good company. Paul writes that he learned to be content in whatever circumstances he found himself, whether in plenty or in want. (See Philippians 4:11–12.) He never judged his spirituality or the spirituality of others by externals. Along with the author of the book of James, Paul taught that suffering could work to good effect in the lives of believers. (See James 1:2–4.)

Great men and women of God down through the centuries understood that true happiness and prosperity come from within and not from without.

CHAPTER 5

COMMANDMENT OR PRINCIPLE?

THERE'S A DELICATE balance here.

And balance is a very difficult thing.

Most of my life as a Christian, I believed tithing was a commandment.

Period. End of story.

Until very recently, I never thought to question the validity of this claim. Once I started to investigate the matter, however, I was forced to take a hard look at what I'd been taught and what I believed.

Historically the theology and practice of the church has been that tithing is a commandment. As I carefully searched the Scriptures, however, I came to another conclusion. Although I believe in and practice tithing, I no longer view the practice as a commandment still binding upon Christians today.

As a pastor of a local church who derives his livelihood from ministry, this personal realization was a bit unnerving. My study of the subject has led me to the following conclusion on this important teaching: I honor tithing as a principle, but I am not required to tithe as a command.

What's the Difference?

What's the difference between a commandment and a principle? A commandment is just that: something we're commanded or required to do. A principle is something we have accepted as truth, and a filter through which we make decisions.

Commandments rest upon law and are to be obeyed, regardless of understanding. A principle rests upon conviction, based on investigation and discovery.

Don't get me wrong; commandments aren't bad. They provide the much-needed boundaries of our lives. We must, however, be careful not to go beyond Scripture, making commandments out of things that are not.

What's done out of legalism won't last, whereas what is done from a heart of personal conviction will. Doing something because you must, fearing the consequences if you don't, is not the basis of a healthy relationship. A person doing something in order to avoid punishment will soon tire and perhaps give up. But a person who loves and is governed by principle will move from strength to strength because the very nature of love is giving and wanting to please the one who is loved.

Is a Principle Binding?

If we accept that tithing is not a commandment that New Testament believers are required to keep, then we must answer this question: "Is a principle binding upon the person who acknowledges its truth?"

Absolutely.

A principle *is* binding, but for very different reasons than obedience to a command. Most of us obey commands because we fear the consequences if we don't. On the other hand, we honor or practice a principle because we have concluded that it represents the right way to act or respond. We choose to embrace a principle, and it holds us or becomes binding because we own it. The truth of the principle has convinced us as to the correct course of action.

You don't hold your convictions, your convictions hold you. Our English term *conviction* is made up of two Latin words that mean, "that by which conquered." A conviction is something that has conquered you, something that governs your thoughts and actions.

Once you have made a decision to embrace the principle of tithing, you're not faced with working through that decision every payday. On the basis of conviction you have made the decision to tithe, so you write the check. It becomes automatic. This decision rests upon the acknowledgement that God owns everything and that you're but a steward; the tithe does not belong to you, but to God.

Writing the check answers the question, "To whom does that belong?" You don't give out of condemnation or in response to crisis. You give out of conviction of the principle.

You obey a commandment, but you honor a principle.

Pay or Give?

Do we *pay* our tithe to the Lord, or do we give it? As we've already discussed, Jesus spoke often about money and riches, but nowhere did He restate the command to tithe. Some would disagree with me here, citing that Jesus did command His followers to tithe in Matthew 23:23. Here's how it reads in the King James Version:

> Woe unto you, scribes and Pharisees, hypocrites! for ye pay tithe of mint and anise and cummin, and have omitted the

weightier matters of the law, judgment, mercy, and faith: these
ought ye to have done, and not to leave the other undone.

The traditional view, based on Matthew 23:23 in the King James,
is that you pay your tithes.

The word translated as "pay" in this translation, however, can
also be translated *give*, as in the NIV. Other contemporary translations don't use either term, simply using "tithe" as a verb. *"For you
tithe mint and dill and cumin..."*

As anyone who has been involved in translation can attest, it
isn't always easy. Part of the difficulty lies in the fact that a one-to-
one correspondence of a specific word doesn't always exist from
one language to another. In addition, most words have a range of
meanings. Such is the case of the Greek word *apodekatoo*, used in
the original and translated in the King James Version as "pay."

One meaning of the word indicates that you pay your tithe
as you would pay any creditor, so translating the word as "give"
doesn't go far enough.

Both translations of the word are correct in that they are faithful
to the semantic range of the meaning of the original word. The
various contemporary English translations reflect this range.
A look at the parallel passage in Luke 11:42 uses the same word
translated as either "pay" or "give." Why is this important? If Jesus
said, "pay," then it would be a commandment. If He said, "give,"
then we are talking about a principle.

To adopt the position that tithing is a commandment, however,
Jesus would have had to state clearly that tithing was a part of His
new covenant. And though He had many opportunities to do just
that, He never did. Whatever your view on the subject, tithing
as a commandment restated in the New Testament is not clear
"beyond a reasonable doubt". Because the Greek is not definitive
and is subject to debate, Matthew 23:23 cannot be used as unques-

tionable proof that Jesus, and thus the New Testament, requires a person to "pay" their tithe.

Most people who hold the conviction that tithing is a commandment go back to Moses to make their case. But as we saw earlier, the practice of tithing actually began with Abraham. Abraham did not tithe to Melchizedek because an external law required it. Abraham tithed to the priest of Salem out of honor and respect for God Most High. The patriarch acknowledged God's help in the battle against the alliance of kings, and his actions give a splendid example of the partnership between God and His people.

Given or Owed?

Many who hold the view that tithing is mandatory and compulsory would teach that a person can't give an offering *until* the whole tithe has been paid.

Here's an example. If I owe you money, I can't give you a monetary gift until I've paid you what I owe. I'm sure that all of us have had the experience of lending money to someone in apparent need, only to watch in dismay as they spend "our money" on other things before they've paid us what they owed.

Does this scenario apply to our relationship with God? Again, it depends on what position we take. If we adopt the position that we pay God our tithe, then we *owe* Him our tithe. If we believe that tithing is a principle and not a command, then we don't *owe* Him; we give our tithes because we have embraced the principle of tithing, not out of obedience to a commandment.

We give out of a heart of love and gratitude to a God who has done everything for us.

Taking a hard stance on the position that "you can't give an offering until you have paid your tithe" would also assume that a person has a certain knowledge base. A Christian who hasn't heard about tithing or understood the principle may give an offering of love from his heart. Remember, an offering is freely given. A more mature or more knowledgeable Christian might cause deep offense to a fellow believer by negating a gift of love with the insistence that "you can't give until you have paid your tithe in full".

Bingo, Anyone?

Tithing is God's way of funding His work here on earth. Because many don't know about or practice tithing, churches may feel compelled to resort to a variety of methods to support their operations—some biblical, and some not. Evangelical believers tend to look down their noses at churches that use things such things as bingo games or raffles to support the work of the Lord.

But are those who criticize any better?

Just look at some of the major Christian publications to see the many get-rich-quick schemes that exist within Christian circles.

The reality is: churches feel the need to hold fundraisers because not all members and adherents honor God with their tithes and offerings. Fundraising can be a good thing, like a capital campaign. People participate because they want to help. Such efforts to raise money for the cause of Christ can be good if they don't take the place of teaching people to tithe as a regular part of their worship to God.

Raising money will often be a one-time event, whereas embracing and practicing stewardship lasts for a lifetime. Yes, there will be times of special need. But I argue that if everyone in our churches understood and practiced tithing, there would be more than enough to do all that we need to do in spreading the gospel.

The truth is, God doesn't "need" us at all.

He is the All-Sufficient One. He does, however, desire to be in relationship with us. And there are certain requirements of relationship. God wants our love and obedience. By tithing, we are reminded that He is our source and our provider. The Hebrew name, *Jehovah Jireh*, means "God will provide" and is one of several names for God. By honoring Him in this way, we express our love for Him and contribute toward His work here on earth.

God needs nothing from us. He has, however, invited us into partnership with Him. He has chosen to depend on His people to meet the physical and financial requirements for His church. Throughout human history God's work has required support through people. Just look at the construction of the tabernacle and the temple in the Old Testament. And the book of Acts records the taking of collections and the sharing of resources in the life of the early churches. This type of giving both honors God and strengthens community among the believers.

Just think about what could be accomplished for the Kingdom of God if everyone understood and embraced the principle of tithing. I love sports and especially enjoy tuning in on the Super Bowl in January. Over the last few years I've found myself dreaming about what our local church—or the greater church of Jesus Christ—could do with the millions of dollars it takes to put on a halftime show that entertains people for twenty minutes and is forgotten by the middle of the third quarter.

Financial shortfalls in local churches don't happen because of God's lack of provision, but because of the unwillingness of God's people to put Him first and honor Him with their tithes and offerings.

A Christian wants to give and see God's work go forward. I suggest ten percent would be the *minimum* that believers would give once they have adopted a giving spirit.

Conviction, Not Crisis

One reason that people both inside and outside of the church are so resistant to hearing about money is the many excesses and abuses they have witnessed within the church. The usual pattern of a pastor is to talk about money only when there's a financial crunch, instead of teaching people about the principle of tithing as a normal part of their walk with God. In addition, we have all witnessed the impassioned appeals of media ministers asking for more financial support from people who have good hearts and often very little cash, while the ministers live in the lap of luxury.

When you give out of conviction, you give during the times of want as well as the times of plenty. Giving becomes a part of your lifestyle, impacted less and less by external circumstances.

Churches, even strong ones, can go through times of financial pressure that stretch their faith. Everyone should be sensitive to those times of need that represent extraordinary circumstances. Churches, as well as individuals, must weather such seasons of financial trial. When they come, it's time for church leaders to step up with clear communication and an outline of the need at hand. After that it's time to look to heaven, trusting God—and God at work in His people—to provide what's necessary.

The Problem of Manipulating

Manipulation usually involves maneuvering someone to do what you want for your benefit, not theirs.

I don't know of anyone, young or old, who likes it.

Church leaders easily fall prey to the temptation to manipulate in the area of finances. Too many people have been burned by high power tactics used to tug on a person's heart strings by manufacturing a crisis. Others use shame in a feeble attempt to sustain the funding for ministry. I know of one church in my own community that locked the doors on a Sunday morning and wouldn't unlock them until they had enough in the offering plates to meet the budget. (Yes, truth is stranger than fiction.)

One not-so-subtle form of manipulation is condemnation, making a person feel bad for not doing something. Condemnation accesses people's feelings of guilt. This type of appeal deliberately plays on the emotions: "If you don't give, then people will be lost and go to hell." Some people will respond to this kind of appeal, but later have feelings of resentment. They will feel uncomfortable and unhappy about something that should make them feel blessed and fulfilled.

I believe guilt—real guilt—is a God-given gift that helps us realize when we've sinned and prompts us to seek forgiveness and make things right. But there is false guilt, too. False guilt overcomes people when someone tries to make them feel bad or responsible for something that is not their fault or tied to their actions. Some people have been raised in this type of environment and are extremely susceptible to manipulation through such means.

False guilt is just that—false. It *feels* like guilt, but it is really just the product of human manipulation to make us feel bad and to motivate us to do something we might not otherwise do.

As followers of God we give out of love and obedience, not because of someone's attempt to make us feel guilty.

The only protection against this type of spiritual abuse is discernment, coupled with research of the ministries to which we give. Any organization, Christian or secular, which operates with integrity, will sustain scrutiny. The following questions need to be asked: (1) "Are the monies collected actually applied to the project they were collected for?" (2) "What percentage of the monies raised actually funds the project?" (3) "Does this ministry publish financial statements for accountability?"

Investing Versus Crisis Giving

Each generation has its own triggers. Impassioned pleas from ministries in financial crises, real or contrived, do *not* motivate Baby Boomers. As a Boomer myself, I respond to the idea of investing rather than giving out of duty or to avert a crisis. I want to be a part of something that's making an impact, something I perceive as a success. From my observation and experience the Gen-Xers and the Millennium Kids feel that same way, but even more strongly.

People want to invest in a winner. They want to see a good return on their investments. What does this look like in the church world? It looks like people coming to know Jesus as personal Savior, experiencing changed lives, and developing strong marriages and families.

Individuals and governments tend to underestimate the work and value of a church that is truly fulfilling its mandate. How can you calculate the financial and social savings of solid marriages and children who are being trained in the ways of godliness instead of merely growing up like weeds?

Leaders of the church need to make certain that they celebrate successes. Sometimes miracles and life changes are the best kept secrets within the local church. By contrast, media ministries are very quick to trumpet what God is doing in and through their organization. No wonder people want to invest in these ministries. Most people want to make a difference and be part of something larger than themselves and is successful in doing what their heart tells them has lasting impact and value.

Grace or Law?

Any discussion about tithing must be seen against the backdrop of the tension between grace and law. Many people balk at the whole concept of tithing, fleeing to the "grace" argument whenever the subject arises. They point to the truths that salvation is by God's grace alone and the free gift of salvation was purchased by Jesus' sacrificial death upon the cross—the ultimate payment for the penalty of sin. Many people say, "We are no longer required to keep the Mosaic Law because Jesus came to set us free from it."

They are right.

And they are wrong.

Yes, we are saved by grace and not by works of the Law. But salvation isn't the only issue in these few years God gives us to walk this earth. Once we've been rescued from hell and an empty, purposeless life, the driving force of our existence—the reason we get up in the morning—is to please the One who laid down His life for us.

We need to beware of the human tendency to succumb to pitfalls. There is the legalism ditch. The legalist takes an extreme position, requiring tithing as a commandment. You don't want to fall into that ditch. But there's another one. The other ditch is an approach that says we're saved and that's all that matters. This type of thinking can lead Christians to believe that obedience and personal holiness are unimportant.

We don't want to fall into that ditch, either.

Actually, Satan doesn't care to which extreme he pushes us. His goal is to keep us from God's blessing, and a ditch is a ditch.

We need to find the balance between what Jesus did for us, our salvation and right standing with God, and our service to Him through living a life that is pleasing and fruitful while on earth. The "Good News" should touch every area of our lives, including our finances.

Balance, as I said, is a very difficult thing.

CHAPTER 6

PRINCIPLES OF THE KINGDOM

G OD CAN'T MULTIPLY what we don't sow.

Principles seem to have gone out of style.

We don't hear much these days about living life governed by eternal truths. Most people in our contemporary society no longer think in terms of moral absolutes. They see principles as outdated and irrelevant in an age of moral and ethical relativity.

"After all," they will tell you, "I have my truth, and you have yours."

In the eyes of many today truth is adaptable, shifting with the circumstances. You can take it off or put it on like a jacket.

Situational ethics recognizes no absolute right or wrong. True to its name, the situation determines the appropriate response separate from any acknowledged moral law—"it all depends." This grows out of the philosophical system that denies the existence of God. If there is no God, then there is no ultimate authority to whom everyone will one day be required to give an account. And where there are no rules, chaos reigns.

We live in an age very much like that described in Judges 21:25 (NKJV), where "everyone did what was right in his own eyes." Spend just a little time in this Old Testament book and you'll quickly note the moral sewer that people gravitate to when left to indulge their own selfish and sinful desires.

In stark contrast to this bleak scene, the Christian life is built upon and governed by principles that exist beyond the human realm and originate with God.

Jesus and the Kingdom

Jesus used principles to teach people how to order their lives. He taught His disciples about the laws of His kingdom. Jesus used the phrase "kingdom of God" often in His teaching, and His audience knew instinctively what He meant. A kingdom has a king, and it's assumed that the subjects of that kingdom will honor its laws.

As citizens of this kingdom, we should act and respond in a way that represents the kingdom of God. We base our decisions on our service to our King.

Jesus communicated this spiritual truth by telling His followers they were to be "in the world but not part of the world." (See John 17.) When Jesus stood before Pilate, exhausted by the hours of torture and interrogation and beaten to the point of death, He still spoke with the authority of a king. "My kingdom is not of this world," He told the governor (John 18:36).

Jesus' powerful declaration rattled Pilate, the representative of the earthly superpower of Rome, and he desperately sought for a way to release Jesus. He recognized the spiritual authority—the *other worldliness*—resident in this Man, even though he couldn't quite grasp it.

If such spiritual principles or laws of the eternal kingdom of God exist, then they will be as true today as when they were penned. Because they are eternal, we can't bend or adjust them to suit us and still expect the law or principle to work for us in the way God intended. Here's a starting list of some of these principles of God's kingdom:

The Principle of Sowing and Reaping

In Mark 4:3–20 Jesus told the story of a man who went out to sow seed on his land. Scattering the same seed in various types of soil across his property, he ended up with very different results.

Some of the seed fell on shallow, rocky soil and didn't have the depth of soil necessary for the plant to grow to maturity. Some fell among the thorns, which Jesus likened to the cares and deceitfulness of earthly riches, which choked off the new life. Even the seed that fell upon good soil yielded different amounts of increase: 30, 60, 100 times what was originally sown.

God can't multiply what we don't sow. Paul underscored this truth, saying, "Whoever sows sparingly will also reap sparingly, and whoever sows generously will also reap generously" (2 Cor. 9:6).

I once heard a self-made millionaire give a teaching on a corollary of sowing and reaping. He had us turn to the opening chapter of Genesis where he pointed out that every living thing reproduces after its own kind. (See Genesis 1:11–12.) You get the idea; apple trees produce apples, rabbits produce rabbits. This man believed that one reason for the failure of people's business ventures and investments is that they use their tithe money for investments or to start a business instead of honoring God with their finances. In effect, they "plant" their tithes in the kingdom of this world and expect it to bear fruit in the kingdom of God.

What was his point? The spiritual seed of the tithe only bears fruit when planted in the spiritual soil for which it was intended. You can't plant one type of seed and expect a different crop in the natural world, nor in the spiritual one.

The Principle of Reciprocity

> Give, and it will be given to you. A good measure, pressed down, shaken together and running over, will be poured into your lap. For with the measure you use, it will be measured to you.
>
> —LUKE 6:38

What an amazing passage! Let's mine some of its riches phrase-by-phrase.

"Give and it will be given to you"

The very nature of the love that comes from God is giving: "For God so loved that He gave...." (John 3:16). What a contrast to the attitude of the world around us that says, "Grab and demand. Look out for yourself."

As we learn to give we become a conduit of God's blessings to others—and have the added joy of opening the doors for God to bless us. This should never be our motive, but it *is* a positive consequence operating by the principles of a very different economy—the economy of the "Kingdom".

"Good measure"

"Good measure" simply means *full*. I remember being at church picnics as a child. When it came to the ice cream time, my friends and I would watch very closely, making sure we got into the line of the person scooping out the biggest portions.

To be honest, I still do this.

I want all that's coming to me and nothing less.

Our human tendency is to want more and to "cheat" a little on the portion served or delivered to someone else. Solomon had something to say about that inclination:

The LORD abhors dishonest scales, but accurate weights are
his delight.

—PROVERBS 11:1

God requires payment in full measure for what people receive.
That's how He wants us to deal with others. And that's how He
wants to deal with us: in full measure. Make no mistake; God
wants us to experience the fullness of His glory.

And I pray that you, being rooted and established in love, may
have power, together with all the saints, to grasp how wide
and long and high and deep is the love of Christ, and to know
this love that surpasses knowledge—that you may be filled to
the measure of all the fullness of God.

—EPHESIANS 3:17–19

"Pressed down"

The phrase "pressed down" refers to how merchants in Jesus'
day measured out dates or figs in the marketplace. By nature soft
and squishy, these fruits can be compacted easily. In this case the
vendor not only filled the receptacle, but actually pressed down
upon the contents to make room for more.

Jesus said this is how God wants to give to His children.

"Shaken together"

In this scenario the vendor shakes the receptacle to compact
what's being measured and create even more room. How very
different in both practice and spirit this is from the norm, where
the seller is consumed with squeezing out every penny of his own
profit. In the metaphor our Lord uses here, the vendor is generous,
desiring to give the customer added value. That's what God wants
to do for us.

"Running over"

The idea here is that the giver pours out more than the buyer's vessel can even hold! In other words, you fill up the grocery sack until it's bursting. The vessel isn't just full; it's overflowing. As with the previous phrases illustrating this law of reciprocity, "running over" is a picture of how God the Father wants to give to you and me. Paul understood this desire of God to give over and beyond our wildest dreams. "Now to him who is able to do immeasurably more than all we ask or imagine, according to his power that is at work within us" (Eph. 3:20).

This brings to mind the story of the poor widow and God's miraculous provision from 2 Kings 4. The woman was in danger of having her sons sold into slavery because of a crushing debt she had no way of repaying. There were no lines of credit or legal ways of forestalling this horrible possibility. In desperation, she turned to the prophet Elisha for help.

The man of God instructed the widow to bring all the pots, cups, and jars in her home—the more the better. She obeyed his directive and even went from house to house borrowing all the containers she could obtain.

Elisha instructed her to pour out what she had: a seemingly small container of oil. As she poured the oil, the miracle of multiplication took place. Her part was obedience and faith. The oil continued to flow as long as there were vessels to contain it. She had a need, and God used what she had to meet the need.

I wonder how often we miss this type of outpouring of God's love and provision because we have limited room or capacity. At so many levels we don't have enough vessels, either physical or spiritual, to contain the blessing God wants to bestow.

In many cases our receiving requires faith in the unseen and in His ability to intervene supernaturally on our behalf. Where there is no room for risk, there is no room for faith.

I came of age in the 1970s. I had the privilege of observing first-hand the wonderful fresh outpouring of God's Spirit that took place early in that decade. It was also an era of new music, inspiring renewed worship and praise across the continent. Though well meaning and capturing a partial spiritual truth, some of the songs from that period actually limited our spiritual understandings. One such song was "Fill My Cup, Lord."[1]

Do you remember that one? The song certainly communicates a sense of openness to the Lord and acknowledges the need of being filled with His power. But in another sense the picture this chorus paints actually limits our understanding of what God desires to do in our lives.

Let me explain. As we reflect on the word *vessels*, two different types come to mind. First there is a cup, bucket, jar, or some other kind of container. When it's empty it needs to be refilled. But there are also blood vessels that contain something and channel it from one place to another, constantly emptied and continuously filled.

We need to see ourselves as blood vessels, filled on a continuous basis and ready to communicate life and strength to any one in need. Too many of us see ourselves as teacups when we need to see ourselves as fire hoses directing the living water to dowse the destructive fires of hell unleashed in our world. That's what Jesus did.

"For with the measure you use, it will be measured to you."

In other words, what goes around comes around.

How you give is how it will be given to you.

The applications of this principle are almost endless and cover much more than finances. As you give you open up spiritual channels for God to give back to you. Ultimately, God is our source, period. He is the one who repays "shaken down, pressed together." This repayment doesn't always announce itself. We need to look with eyes of faith to see His blessing and provision reaching our lives in a variety of ways. Sometimes the source seems supernatural, with no apparent rhyme or reason. These are the serendipities we experience along the way; if we aren't paying attention, we can miss them as God's repayment.

We should never attribute God's generous dealings in our life as "chance" or "luck."

Understanding the law of reciprocity doesn't mean that we give to get. Receiving is the natural reward of practicing this wonderful law of the kingdom. Any teaching that emphasizes giving to get is a perversion of all that Jesus taught. He lived and modeled that we give of our resources and ourselves because we love and desire to bless others, not for personal gain. We give because we acknowledge God's ownership and lordship over all that we have and so that His kingdom can be advanced here on earth.

The Principle of Multiplication

The feeding of the five thousand in John 6:5–14 stars one of the unsung heroes of the New Testament: Andrew, the brother of Simon Peter.

Let's set the stage. A large number of people had followed Jesus to a fairly remote area. Concerned for their physical well-being, Jesus asked Philip, the practical disciple, "How shall we feed all these people?" While Philip was shaking his head and explaining how it couldn't be done, Andrew quietly found a young boy with a small lunch consisting of five barley loaves and two small fish and brought him to Jesus. Barley was the grain of the common people, so this boy gave out of his own need and not out of his abundance.

Why did Andrew do this? Why bring such a ridiculously small amount of food to Jesus when the need was mind-bendingly large? Andrew obviously had faith that Jesus could and would do something. Yes, he did provide himself with an escape route by adding "but how far will they go among so many?" Even so, he had taken a step of faith that was about to pay incredible dividends.

Jesus, of course, could have created something out of nothing right on the spot. Instead, He chose to use and multiply what someone had brought to Him. Jesus had the people sit down. After looking toward heaven and blessing the little lunch, He instructed His disciples to start passing out the provision. Everyone ate all they could eat. The twelve baskets of food left over underlined God's desire to give over and above what we need. Little became much when placed in the Master's hand.

The Principle of the Laborer

Though spiritually-minded, Jesus was infinitely practical as well. He gave specific instructions to those He sent out to proclaim His kingdom regarding the issue of their room and board. "Stay in that house, eating and drinking whatever they give you, for the worker deserves his wages" (Luke 10:7).

Jesus endorsed the principle that those engaged in spreading the gospel were entitled to have their material needs met by those who benefited from their ministry.

Paul addressed this issue as well. He instructed the churches under his care to remunerate their vocational leaders to the best of their abilities. The leaders also had a responsibility to discharge their duties in a manner worthy of the Lord. Such leaders were deserving of double honor. (See 1 Timothy 5:17–18.)

Have you ever worked two jobs? Most of us have had to do that at least once in our lives. Maybe you can remember how challenging that was—physically and emotionally draining.

That's the way it is for pastors who have to shepherd a flock as well as work out in the marketplace to provide for their families.

Pastors who can receive their entire support from the churches they lead can use all of their time to build and strengthen the body of Christ, instead of trying to juggle competing interests.

Paul is clear that leadership is a gift and that those who have it must lead with diligence. (See Romans 12:8.) But if the shepherd has responsibility, then so do the sheep! Those who benefit from godly leadership have the responsibility to follow their leaders and to provide for their material needs. First Corinthians 9:7–14 speaks for itself: (1) no soldier serves at his own expense and (2) the one who sows and the one who reap both enjoy the fruit of the harvest. Paul asks the rhetorical question, "If we have sown spiritual seed among you, is it too much if we reap a material harvest from you?" (v. 11).

A few words need to be said here. People in vocational ministry are not somehow "more important" than those they lead. Every member of the body of Christ has equal value and is called to minister.

As the pastor of a local church, I acknowledge that we couldn't do church without volunteers, and that no local church could possibly pay those who volunteer for all they do. There are some, however, whom God has gifted to lead and teach within the body. Such gifts in people should be self-evident. These people can be more effective in these tasks as their full-time responsibility, without the added pressure of another job.

People in vocational ministry should be paid not only to "do ministry," but also to create more ministry. These leaders need to give themselves to releasing people to be all they can be. This will involve discovering the unique giftings within a given flock, encouraging and developing those God-given abilities; and then deploying them to see the gospel penetrate a community, a region, and the world.

One reason for the backlash against the professional clergy is that many have postured themselves as kings who are at the top of the heap. They have forgotten that ministry is all about serving—not about being served. (See Matthew 20:28.) Spiritual leaders exist for the people, not the other way around. If ministry only happens when you get a paycheck, then all you really have is a job.

The Principle Linking Heart and Treasure

When you have to create rules to govern human behavior, there can never be enough. This is what makes living a life based upon principles so appealing. Following God is all about heart. Human conduct is best governed from the inside, from the heart. And a thankful heart is a giving heart.

I once saw a cartoon depicting a man being baptized in water by immersion. His whole body was under the water except his hand, above the water, clutching his wallet. When God has our heart He has everything else, including our wallet.

Jesus had much to say about the link between the heart and giving. "Do not store up for yourselves treasures on earth, where moth and rust destroy, and where thieves break in and steal. But store up for yourselves treasures in heaven, where moth and rust do not destroy, and where thieves do not break in and steal. For where your treasure is, there your heart will be also" (Matt. 6:19–21).

I like to invert this last verse by saying, "Where your heart is, there will your treasure be also."

What's really important to someone? Where is a person's treasure? You can quickly discover an individual's true priorities by observing three things: calendar, checkbook, and conversation. Take a look at where people spend their time. Check where they spend their money. Listen to what people talk about and note where they pour their energies.

Where you spend your time and money and what you talk about reveals the true content of your heart. Actions speak louder than words. People can repeatedly affirm that something is important to them, but if their time and money don't flow to their stated values, how would you ever know it?

One of Dr. Steven Covey's *Seven Habits of Highly Effective People* is the principle of "putting first things first."[2] To illustrate this point in a lecture he gave, the bestselling author had a volunteer from the audience come forward. He gave the man some large rocks, then instructed him to fit them into a container already three-quarters full of smaller rocks. But it was impossible. Try as he might, the man couldn't squeeze the large rocks in after the fact. But when Dr. Covey put the same large rocks in the same container first, the smaller rocks found their place around the larger rocks, making room for both.

That's how it works with our finances. Put first things first. Honor God by writing your tithe check before paying a single bill.

The Principle of Asking

Who could state this principle more succinctly than the apostle James? "You do not have, because you do not ask God" (James 4:2). Many Christians do without or live at a level much lower than necessary because they don't ask the Father for what they need. Of course God *knows* what we need. He knows everything! But God is always looking for a relationship with His children, and He wants us to ask. This accomplishes at least two things: we talk to Him, and we come to recognize God as our true source.

Jesus encouraged His followers to ask the Father for their needs, as illustrated in what we know as "The Lord's Prayer." (See Matthew 6:9–13.)

The prayer must have been startling to the disciples from the very beginning. Jesus instructed them to address the God of the Universe as "our Father." Speaking in Aramaic, as He did, He must have used the word *abba*. The word *daddy* comes as close as anything to describing this term of family closeness and endearment.

Jesus taught us to look to God the Father as the source of our provision. "Give us this day our daily bread" (Matt. 6:11, NKJV). For the average North American bread isn't very exciting. But for the first-century inhabitant of Palestine, bread was basic to life itself. Asking for bread represented asking and trusting God for the most basic of needs.

In the Sermon on the Mount Jesus was even more specific, saying, "Ask and it will be given to you; seek and you will find; knock and the door will be opened to you. For everyone who asks receives; he who seeks finds; and to him who knocks, the door will be opened" (Matt. 7:7–8). The tense of the verbs *ask*, *seek*, and *knock* in the original Greek communicates the idea of "keep asking, keep seeking, and keep knocking."

In this passage Jesus gave us permission to ask as often as we have need. Just because you asked yesterday or last week doesn't mean you can't ask today. The Father doesn't grow tired of responding to the requests of His children. "If your earthly fathers being evil know how to give you good gifts, how much more will the heavenly Father give to those who ask." (See Matthew 7:11.)

Confidence in asking is a direct function of relationship. When you have a belief that the person you are asking not only has the resources but the desire to share them, asking becomes much easier.

James 4:3 declares that what we have is to be used for His Kingdom and purposes, not for our fleshly pursuits and pleasures. We are to ask for the right reason: to extend the kingdom of God and not feather our own nests.

Sometimes Father God wants to bless us, not because we ask, but just because He loves us and delights in us. My earthly father did this for me. My hometown prided itself on its high school band. I took advantage of free instruction in learning to play the trombone from grade five onward. All along the way my parents provided me with the very best instrument they could afford. I eventually ended up with a nice professional quality symphony horn. It was good, but it wasn't the best.

One weekend, just a month or so before the end of my junior year in high school, I was chosen to play in a state select band at the University of Akron. My parents drove from Dover to Akron to hear me play. During the concert my father observed that the other players all had a certain model of trombone. The next week he called me out to the car and opened the trunk. There was a brand new trombone of the finest quality. The one that I had was really just fine, but my dad wanted me to have the best. He wanted to show me in a tangible way that he loved me.

Almost three decades later I still play that horn in church, and I remember how my father, out of love for me, decided to bless me just because he wanted to bless me. Our heavenly Father is like that, too.

The Principle of Faith

Faith can't be separated from any discussion of stewardship and provision. As with other foundational concepts the teaching on faith has often been skewed and manipulated almost beyond recognition. A balanced understanding of faith, however, is crucial in constructing a solid and workable theology of money and its proper place in the life of the believer. Christians need to have faith in God and not faith in their faith. (See Mark 11:22.)

I have lived long enough as a Christian to see swings of emphasis within the church. In the 1970s we saw a renewed interest in faith. It was good. It was needed. But when taken to an extreme, anything can be destructive. We saw people, in the name of faith, naming and claiming all sorts of things.

"I'm a King's kid."

"I deserve the very best."

"I'll give my three bedroom ranch house to God in exchange for a five bedroom mansion."

This type of confession is nothing more than selfishness dressed up in religious garb.

The problem with the "faith message" is that its teaching contains a certain amount of truth, making it difficult to refute. But its emphasis is in the wrong place. The error comes when people have faith in their faith instead of faith in God.

Paul was a man of faith and learned how to live in plenty or in want. The status of his earthly possessions had nothing to do with his prosperity.

Daniel 3 contains a powerful story that helps put the whole faith issue into perspective. Nebuchadnezzar, king over the mighty Babylonian empire, constructed a towering image and, at a certain signal, required everyone to bow down in worship to this idol.

Three young Hebrew men, Shadrach, Meshach, and Abednego, taken by the Babylonians upon the conquest of Jerusalem and groomed to be leaders, refused to bow down—even though they knew the penalty for such resistance. Though it most likely would mean their own death, these young men refused to bend their knees to the king's idol.

In their exchange with the king recorded in Daniel 3:17–18, we see a great spiritual truth that epitomizes a correct application of faith. They declared that the God they served was able to deliver them out of the hand of Nebuchadnezzar. However, even if He did not do so for some reason unknown to them, they would not bow down or serve the golden image. In the midst of a life-threatening circumstance, they refused to dictate to God Almighty what He should do.

What a healthy pattern for our prayers. God wants us to pray in accordance with His will and purposes; which, I might add, aren't always in line with what we, in our weakness and limited under-standing, think should happen.

We aren't God.

We aren't all-knowing.

We don't see the big picture.

And God is not bound to do what *we* think best. We need to submit in love and trust that He, and He alone, knows what will be best for us and for furthering His kingdom. We pray, believe, and exercise faith. But we trust in the goodness, omniscience, and omnipotence of God. We allow God to be God, acknowledging that His ways are higher than our ways.

I don't know about you, but I am greatly comforted in the knowl-edge that I serve a God who knows more than I do.

The Principle of Faithfulness

Let's revisit an important parable of Jesus we looked at earlier in the book.

Our Lord's story of the three stewards in Matthew 25:14–30 not only teaches good stewardship, but it also contains the kingdom principle of faithfulness. It shows us how taking care of the seemingly few things entrusted into our care paves the way for being "ruler" over more.

Why would anyone give someone more to oversee when they're not even handling what they presently have?

We all know people in positions of leadership or stewardship who are in way over their heads. In the business world this is referred to as the "Peter Principle": people tend to be promoted to the level of their incompetence. Employees rise up through the ranks until they finally reach the outside limits of their abilities. And that is where they stay, mired in jobs beyond their capabilities.

God doesn't work like that, and neither does His kingdom. God desires to increase our influence, but He has many ways of doing that. And He will never destroy us in the process. As we learn to be good stewards in smaller areas, we acquire the skills necessary to be trusted with more. This development is a constant and continuous process. He has a plan for our life, and though it is always good, it's not always easy. Each test and opportunity that comes our way is a chance to find out about our abilities, our limitations, and where we need to rely upon God.

In the parable of the stewards, we see the master giving of his resources to see if these men could handle their responsibilities. Two of these men used their talents wisely and were given more. The third hid his talent. Instead of receiving more, even the one he had been given was stripped from him.

One question about this story has plagued me. Why was it that two of the stewards had the confidence to invest what was given— even risking their talents—when the third was so fearful that he hid his in the ground? As I meditated upon this story, I received this insight. The words of the third steward contain the answer to this question:

> Then the man who had received the one talent came. 'Master,' he said, 'I knew that you are a hard man, harvesting where you have not sown and gathering where you have not scattered seed. So I was afraid and went out and hid your talent in the ground. See, here is what belongs to you.
>
> —MATTHEW 25:24–25

It comes down to relationship and trust. This man didn't know the master and didn't understand the master's heart, his resulting actions reflecting this warped view. In the end the master became to the third steward what the man had judged him to be: a hard man, a fearsome man. The third man's skewed perspective became the basis of his judgment.

The Principle of Use

The story of the three stewards also communicates the principle of the law of use: what we use increases, and what we don't use we lose. The two faithful stewards put the master's money to work, investing what had been given them. The five talents multiplied and became ten, the three became six. The third steward buried the talent given to him. It gained nothing. In the end of the story, the master took the one talent and gave it to the one who had the ten. This seems unfair, unless you understand the principle.

We can observe this dynamic in many areas of life, whether we apply it to physical strength or some type of artistic expression.

Athletes certainly know this law. They train countless hours to strengthen their muscles and hone their skills. Musicians understand the law perfectly. Even the most gifted musicians begin by learning their instruments. As any parent of a band student can attest, this start-up phase can be painful to the ears. But as each hour of practice passes, the noise begins to give way to music as the musician becomes more proficient. It's the law of use.

Anyone who has ever broken a limb understands the truth of this principle. The medical profession immobilizes the damaged arm or leg by putting on a cast. The broken bone heals, but creates weakness in the arm or leg because it's not being used.

The limb atrophies.

It shrinks noticeably in size and strength.

The only way to restore those muscles, returning them to a pre-injury condition, is by exercising. By use.

David's pre-royal job as shepherd illustrates this principle. During the long periods of inactivity and boredom, David used those downtimes to hone his skills with a sling. Who knows how many countless rocks he hurled at an unspecified number of targets? With each stone he became more proficient with this weapon. Those hours of practice would one day come in handy when he faced the giant, Goliath. As David stood there in the valley with the enemy towering over him, what do you think he prayed? For a miracle? I think it's more likely he prayed that his aim, honed into a fine skill, would not fail him.

As David faithfully cared for his father's sheep, developing his proficiency with a sling through long, lonely days, God knew that very skill would one day change the man's life forever.

When you're walking step by step with the God of eternity, there's no such thing as wasted time.

CHAPTER 7

NEED OR WANT?

A CONSUMER MENTALITY CONSUMES you.
We speak of "needs." But what is a need? What is a want?

The affluence of North America greatly complicates that question. No people in the history of the earth have had more materially, or enjoyed it less.

When you travel in poorer parts of the world, you come home with a heartfelt appreciation for the many blessings that we enjoy every day of our lives, and mostly take for granted. Even though too many in our society live at or below the poverty line, we have unprecedented opportunities to advance ourselves and social safety nets that most of the world can only dream about.

Yet instead of being grateful, we too often complain about what we lack. Even in a land of plenty we think we deserve more. In the process we begin to confuse our wants for our needs.

When the Line Blurs

We have a need for water, for food, and for a roof over our heads.
Those things are simply the basics of life on planet earth.
Having something to drink is a need; having a vanilla latte is not.

Having something to eat is a need; having a steak is not.

Having a place to lay your head is a need; living in a mansion is not.

Our very economy in North America is built upon creating "need" in people's lives. Advertisers play upon our selfishness, envy, and insecurity. We feel less than adequate unless we have the latest electronic gizmo or the right designer label on our clothes. People buy into the empty promises that happiness can be found in the purchase of the right toothpaste or deodorant.

In our first church we had a couple that constantly struggled with money or, more accurately, the lack of it. During a particularly difficult time they told me they were so discouraged about not having enough money to cover expenses that they went on a mini-holiday to get away from the pressure. They drove to a resort area, rented a hotel room, had a nice meal out, and went to a movie to get their minds off their financial woes.

In their minds this trip was a "need."

The demand for bigger and better pervades almost every aspect of our consumer society. We have bigger, better burgers and super-sized beverages. And have you noticed all the options you can get on a new vehicle? Never mind the options—have you noticed the new vehicles? Bigger is better, and the more money you spend, the better the toy.

Look at the SUV market. The ultimate Sport Utility Vehicle is the Hummer, the civilian version of the Humvee developed for the U.S. military.

These vehicles were made to race into battle across remote dirt tracks and rough terrain. And yet the farthest most Hummer owners ever get "off road" is a neighborhood cul-de-sac.

This bigger-is-better approach can also be seen in the housing market. In the 1950s the average size house in the city in which

I live was 1,200 square feet. It's now 2,100 square feet. How many bathrooms can you use? Where will it end? A friend of mine who sells real estate once referred to houses as "boxes to keep our stuff in." When the box is no longer big enough, then we buy a bigger one to make room for more stuff.

A Consumer Mentality

When VCRs first came out, they were over five hundred dollars and made to be repaired. That is no longer the case. Now you can pick one up with more features than those first models for under a hundred.

Buying a new item instead of fixing the old one may occasionally be the best option of the good steward, but it may also lend itself to a careless attitude about our possessions. "It's no big deal. I'll just buy another one—a better one." Whether one can really afford that new and better item may not even be considered.

"Hey, it's broken," we say. "I need a new one."

I recently came across the following verse in the book of Proverbs:

> Costly treasure and wealth are in the home of a wise person,
> but a fool devours them.
>
> —PROVERBS 21:20, GW

A consumer mentality consumes you.

A consumer mentality says, "It's never enough," no matter how much you have. If one million dollars is good, two million is better. Jesus drove home this point to His disciples: "Watch out! Be on your guard against all kinds of greed; a man's life does not consist in the abundance of his possessions" (Luke 12:15). Following this statement, Jesus told the story of a man who tore down his barns to build bigger ones, only to die the next day and pass into an eternity without God. (See Luke 12:16–32.)

Our Lord had a one-word description of this entrepreneur: fool.

But What About My Needs?

Does God really want to meet my needs? Does God really love me?

In an age of fractured families, the revelation of God as *Father* gets filtered through the lens of dysfunctional and absent fathers who bear no resemblance to the glory and love of the heavenly Father.

This fact hasn't escaped Satan's notice.

Our enemy knows what is spiritually important and goes after those things with a vengeance. He knows that if he can warp people's perception of "father," he can cripple their ability to relate to God the Father.

From the time of the original temptation in the Garden of Eden, Satan has made a frontal attack on the character and nature of God. He planted the seed of doubt in Eve's mind about God's truthfulness, goodness, and motives. The father of lies started his assault with a bit of truth, albeit a half-truth, taken out of context. "Did God really say…?" (See Genesis 3:1.) Once he planted the seed of doubt and deception, he moved in for the kill. You know the rest of the story.

Jesus came to earth to reveal the character and nature of God to mankind, for us to see firsthand the heart of the Father. Jesus said, "I and the Father are one" (John 10:30). Jesus was "God in 3-D."

Trusting in the love and goodness of the Father is critical to our discussion of His provision. We can believe in our heads that God is omnipotent, that He can do anything, including meeting our needs. And we can believe that He wants to meet the needs of others. But what about me? A huge gulf exists between God being able and God *wanting* to meet our needs.

After all, doesn't He have a whole universe to run? Does He really have time to spare for individuals? Does He really care about me?

God is not only capable of doing what He has promised, He *wants* to because He is love. As a parent, I would love to bless my children with financial resources, but I have limitations. I would love to give them each a million dollars. In spite of my desire to bless them in such an extravagant way, that will never happen. It's highly unlikely I will have such resources in the course of my life.

God, on the other hand, has both the will and the power to provide for us. His resources are limitless, and Jesus declares the Father's desire to give us good things. (See Luke 12:32.) He says that if our earthly fathers, who have a fallen and selfish nature, can put their own needs aside out of love for their children, how much more does the heavenly Father desire to give good things to His children and make certain their needs are met. (See Matthew 7:9–11.)

Dialogue With Your Provider

People feel hurt, angry, or disappointed when they think God isn't providing what they expect or feel they deserve. They question the fundamentals. "Is God a good God? Can I trust Him? Is the Bible true when it promises that God will provide for my needs?"

Instead of making the accusation, "God isn't meeting my needs," it may be wise to start by looking at the person who stares back at you when you look in the mirror. Ask yourself these questions:

"Have I been a good steward?

Have I been careless in how I have managed my money?

Have I been living beyond my means?

Do I have excessive expectations that have been shaped by the materialistic society in which I live?"

God is big enough and loving enough to handle your anger. If you find yourself disappointed with His level of provision, tell Him so. But as with all good communication, you must be willing to hear what *He* has to say, too.

When we engage in open dialogue we often discover we haven't seen the whole picture—or that we've missed something crucial to gaining understanding about what's really happening in a particular season of our lives. We can expect that God will help us step back and get a wider, more accurate perspective.

Philippians 4:19 gives us this assurance: "And my God will meet all your needs according to his glorious riches in Christ Jesus." What do the riches in Christ look like to you? Are they material? Spiritual? How would you measure such riches?

The list is truly endless. Here are a few examples. We have been granted the free gift of eternal salvation. We are no longer slaves to sin but are truly the children of God. As children of the King, we are His heirs. His riches include peace of mind and joy that transcends happiness. Knowing that *someone* beyond ourselves is looking out for us brings a deep sense of security and well-being.

In the end, we must once again make a decision to trust Him, His goodness and wisdom, and that He cares for us and knows what's best. We can have an unshakeable faith in both His ability and desire to provide for us.

What Do I Desire?

A friend of mine used to say, "You move towards whatever your eyes are on." You can see this when you're driving. The car tends to drift in the direction you're looking.

The same is true spiritually.

We move toward the things that we desire and that receive our focus. And what are those things? What is it that we truly desire?

David wrote, "Delight yourself in the LORD and he will give you the desires of your heart" (Ps. 37:4–5). We quote this passage, but how do we live it? When our desire is to love the Lord with heart, soul, mind, and strength, when we have put Him first in our lives, then He can safely give us the desires of our heart because they will be *His* desires as well.

A paraphrase of a Saint Augustine quote goes like this: "Please to please God and do anything you please." Augustine wasn't preaching license here—that you can do whatever you want regardless of the consequences. He was saying that God can and will give us the desires of our heart when we put Him first. Our desires are His desires; His desires are our desires.

Any parent instinctively understands this principle. We would give our children the world—but not at the expense of their well-being. We would never want to give them anything that could cause them harm. Remember, God has our ultimate good at the center of all He does for us. He will not give us a gift in the form of talents or resources that would cause us to stray from His path.

Here are two more sometimes-uncomfortable questions: "Do I really need it? Can I live without this thing?" I remember many a Christmas season when my desire for a certain toy was inflamed by slick advertising on television. These toys took on larger-than-life proportions. I would circle them in the Christmas catalog, and I just knew that if I got these things for Christmas, my life would be complete. Now, from the vantage point of adulthood, I remember discarding those same toys after half an hour of fleeting fascination. The real thing seemed diminished from what I'd seen portrayed on TV, and I soon became bored with the toys. The desire to have can eclipse the joy of possessing.

Wrestling With the Green Monster

The Tenth Commandment states, "You shall not covet" (Exod. 20:17). To *covet* means to desire something that belongs to another person, to the point that the desire consumes you.

There's another word for that: *Envy.*

Covetousness, envy, craving, and greed are all related. Envy becomes personal. It goes beyond wanting what someone else has and crosses over into resentment, or even hatred. Envy describes a desire so strong it ensnares you; it becomes an obsession.

The story of David and Bathsheba provides one of the very best examples of the havoc and destruction of covetousness. This is truly the lowest point in the life of an otherwise great man. It reveals so many sins: lack of self-control, lust, self-gratification, deceit, murder, and cover-up. Although David did repent of this heinous deed, the consequences of his sin dogged him for the rest of his life.

In fact, this one act of unrestrained self-indulgence ended up bringing horrible turmoil on his family. The sword did not depart from his household. Trouble and intrigue plagued his reign from that point on, punctuated by the murder of his son Amnon by his other son Absalom, who led a bloody rebellion that almost cost David his kingdom. Like father like son: Absalom coveted his father's kingdom, and it cost him his life. (See 2 Samuel 11–18.)

The sin of covetousness was not limited to David and his family. Joshua 7 recounts the tragic tale of Achan. God made it clear to the Israelites that during the attack on Jericho all of the spoils of battle were under the ban; they were not to take anything from the city. Achan heard this warning along with everyone else, but he didn't heed it. In the heat of the battle Achan gave in to the temptation to take plunder, in direct violation of God's commandment.

His action had dire consequences for the whole spiritual community. When confronted with his sin, Achan confessed. "When I saw in the plunder a beautiful robe from Babylonia, two hundred shekels of silver and a wedge of gold weighing fifty shekels, I coveted them and took them" (Josh. 7:21).

Notice the progression: Achan saw, he coveted, and he took. We are not immune from the sin of Achan. We see, we covet, and we act.

The sin of covetousness can grow secretly within a person's heart, undetected by anyone else, at least initially. Sooner or later, however, this sin will manifest itself to the outside world—as in the cases of David and Achan.

The opposite of being covetous is being content with what we have. (See Philippians 4:11–12.) Instead of envying someone's life or possessions, we celebrate the blessing of the Lord on their lives. This happiness for others guards our hearts from becoming obsessed with what someone else has and allowing "dark thoughts" to take root where no such thoughts belong.

Envy grows out of dissatisfaction with the level of provision we are experiencing. Paul tells us that love does not envy, but rather rejoices in the good fortune and advancement of others.

Cultivate a Thankful Heart

Cultivating a thankful heart is an essential element of sorting out our wants from our needs. Having a thankful heart helps us recognize the things that God has done and is doing. Then, on the basis of His past provision and present kindness, we can have confidence in His future provision.

Our situations may not change, at least not right away. But our perspective will! Instead of complaining about what we don't have, we will recognize the hand of God and His generous dealings in our lives. Instead of grumbling, we open our eyes to what God is doing right now to meet our needs.

He is working. He is providing. He is blessing. He is moving events and people and circumstances, working toward our good.

If we truly open our eyes, we'll see it.

CHAPTER 8

WHY DO WE GIVE?

Having first gained all you can, and secondly, saved all you can, then give all you can give.

—JOHN WESLEY[1]

W HY PEOPLE DO the things they do has always intrigued me. What motivates us? Fear? Duty? Habit? Love? Why I do something is as important as what I do. And if I'm thinking clearly, the "whys" will give direction to the "whats."

Most people in our churches are no longer willing to do something merely because someone else—even someone in authority—"tells" them to do it.

People don't want to be told.

They want to be persuaded, encouraged, or reasoned with, but in the twenty-first century being lectured goes down hard (or not at all). In other words, people today need to do things out of a sense of conviction or choice, not out of duty or obligation.

Why, then, do people give to the work of the Lord?

For many, giving is a genuine expression of love. For others, the motivation might be all about self: giving to get, giving as a way of manipulating, giving to impress others, or giving to feel good.

Correctly discerning the motive behind an action—any action—is a tricky proposition. Why? Because we human beings are masters at covering things up to make ourselves look better. We become so good at it that we even deceive ourselves.

Self-deception, of course, is the ultimate deception, and we need the indwelling Holy Spirit to help us correctly discern and understand the deepest things within our hearts.

The Basic Motive

When it comes to why we do what we do, people who study such things offer up two schools of thought. One school concentrates on behavior: people do what they do because that's how they've been trained. They say you can change a person's external actions through behavior modification, rewarding behavior you wish to see continue and punishing behavior you want to change or modify.

And it works—to a point. You might change behavior, but totally miss changing the heart—the "why." To emphasize external action over the internals of the heart falls way short of true discipleship.

Whether they realize it or not, church leaders sometimes employ this very technique in the name of discipleship. They look for ways to reward and applaud people for behavior they deem desirable. Honoring God with our giving should never be the basis of our acceptance by His church. People who give out of shame or peer pressure to be accepted will soon learn to resent not only the church, but also God.

The other school of thought places emphasis on changing a person's thinking, not their external behavior. It believes that changing how a person *thinks* will translate into a change in how a person acts.

This is in line with the Word of God. "For as he thinks within himself, so he is" (Prov. 23:7, NAS).

Scripture warns us against conforming to this world and its thought processes; we are to be transformed to the thought processes of the Kingdom of God. (See Rom. 12:2.) If we can help people to understand *why* they are to give, it will release them to give with a joyful heart, not out of a spirit of obligation.

"God loves a cheerful giver" (2 Cor. 9:7). If the Holy Spirit, through Paul, encouraged people with these very words, it means that cheerful giving is possible. This type of giving brings joy to God and the giver.

So where are all the cheerful givers? As with so many other areas of our service to God, that which is born of love and conviction can degenerate to a mere form or empty ritual, devoid of any love or relationship.

Doing the Right Thing

I started pastoring at the age of twenty-two. As you might imagine, my youthfulness presented a bit of a challenge for some of the seniors who made up the core of the church. You might say I didn't have an overabundance of credibility at the time.

Across the street and within easy walking distance was a residence for seniors. Occasionally an elderly lady by the name of Mrs. Fish would wander over to our church. This happened one night when we were discussing 2 Corinthians 9:7 and the whole issue of giving. She listened for a few minutes and then declared strongly that if people couldn't give with a cheerful heart, they shouldn't give at all. When I endeavored to gently introduce the concept of doing the right thing because it was the right thing and not based upon feelings, she abruptly stormed out of the room.

Emotions are valid, but they're not always an accurate guide for right actions. I don't know about you, but I don't always "feel" like doing the right or necessary thing. I tell this to our kids all the time. "You may not *feel* like doing the dishes or cleaning up your room, but it still needs to be done."

One of the most effective ways to strengthen our own spiritual maturity is to deliberately override our emotions or internal opposition to doing the right thing, compelling ourselves to line up with what the Spirit is saying. In Galatians 5:17, Paul warns us that our flesh works in direct opposition to God. So why should it surprise us when we will feel like we're swimming against the current by doing the right thing?

Sometimes doing the right thing involves sacrifice. Strangely enough, it is in such moments that we come closest to the heart of worship. From one end of Scripture to the other, it's clear that all true worship requires sacrifice.

So why do I personally tithe? What's my motivation? Am I trying to leverage God to bless me, or seeking to apply some spiritual formula that guarantees financial success? Anything less than "because I love Him and want to serve Him with all that I have" will lead to a very sterile relationship with God.

Just Because?

A pastor for many years, my father has years of perspective. We've discussed numerous times the differences in pastoring in our respective eras. One of the stark contrasts between then and now is people's perception of the authority of those in ministry.

At one time the pastor's word was rarely questioned. People trusted that the minister had heard from God when delivering "the message." In our contemporary culture, people tend to respond to strong teaching with, "Who says?" or maybe, "That's just your opinion."

Then they go and do as they please.

In an environment where people frequently question authority, spiritual leaders need a well-thought-out theology on subjects of importance—including tithing.

"Just because" just won't cut it. (And I have my doubts that such an answer would have worked in my dad's day, either.) We can hope that where people have right hearts, they will respond appropriately to the truth and to the conviction of the Holy Spirit. Then it's up to them to bring their lives into line with what God is saying.

A popular bumper sticker of the sixties and seventies was the two-word declaration Question Authority. The truth is, questioning authority can be good or bad, depending on the situation. We see throughout the Bible the need of having authority figures in our life. This, of course, assumes that the authority is godly, not abusive or self-centered—as we so often see in cults.

Jesus Christ, the ultimate authority, welcomed His disciple's questions. He responded to them when they requested more information, and He did so without making them feel like they'd overstepped their bounds. If God Himself doesn't reproach those who are genuinely inquiring, should we? Let's foster an environment that permits people to ask questions. People gain confidence in this kind of leadership and grow in spiritual maturity as they feel free to ask and to decide for themselves.

While Easter dinner was being prepared, a little girl watched intently as her mother cut two inches off the end of the ham. As they say, "inquiring minds want to know," so the girl asked her mommy why she did this. This stopped her mother in her tracks for a moment. She had to admit that she had no good reason for doing so, other than the fact that *her* mother had always done this.

Now the little girl and her mother both had their interest piqued, so they called up Grandmother.

On being asked the "why" question, the older lady had the same response, "My mother used to do it." Now three generations of people were curious as to the mystery of the ham, so they went to visit Granny. When they inquired of the old woman, she laughed out loud and said, "The reason I cut off the two inches was because my roasting pan was too small."

I wonder if we have a similar reason when it comes to things we do in the name of following God: doing something from tradition rather than careful thought.

What About the Reasons We Give?

Motive deals more with the heart; reasons deal more with the head. Believers want and need to know why they do what they do. Pastors and teachers can help them in the examination stage, backing up the teaching of the church with the clear principles of Scripture.

One of my good friends is an ordained Catholic priest. As you might imagine, he and I have had some lively discussions about spiritual things. However, in one such interaction he made the point that when we share the gospel with people, we're not trying to prove that our faith is logical. We are, however, trying to show that our faith is not illogical.

So what are some good reasons for giving of our tithes and offerings?

Love for God

The highest and best reason for giving to God and others is love for God, period. We give with no ulterior motive, no thought of being seen or applauded by others. For those who try to impress by how much they give, Jesus will say, "You have your reward." (See Matthew 6:5.)

In spite of what you may have heard from some Christian sources, we don't give to get something in return. Have you ever had someone give you something, only later to realize it was a setup? That sort of thing doesn't fly with God. We can't manipulate Him. We can't cut a deal with Him. It won't work to tell Him, "I'll do this for You, God, but I expect You to do this for me."

Authentic love gives freely. Period.

Because we love God, doing what is right and pleasing to Him brings a sense of joy and fulfillment. It's a happy prospect. It's like being in a good marriage, where a husband and wife really like to please and serve each other. In fact, bringing a smile to my wife's face is one of the most joyful things I can do.

Nothing kills relationship more quickly than obligation. If this is true of human relationship, it's also true of our relationship with God. If we love God, we give out of love and not out of compulsion. "You must each make up your own mind as to how much you should give. Don't give reluctantly or in response to pressure. For God loves the person who gives cheerfully" (2 Cor. 9:7, TLB).

Gratitude

When we truly open our eyes to what God has done for us, we will *want* to give because we're overflowing with gratitude. A grateful person will be a thankful person. Christal Clayton summed up this point well. "Our real reason [for giving] should be gratitude to our heavenly Father for His mercy and His gift of salvation. Those who are faithful with their tithes will witness, with one accord, that they have been blessed in all areas of life: socially, financially and spiritually."[2]

Obedience

A major point of this book is my conviction that tithing is a principle and not a commandment.

Wanting to please God and do what He has asked of us is not a legalistic adherence to an endless set of rules and laws, but the highest expression of love. Jesus said, "If you love Me, keep my commandments" (John 14:15, NKJV). First John 5:3 says, "This is love for God: to obey his commands. And his commands are not burdensome [oppressive]."

Honoring God with our lives and our resources, then, is both a principle *and* a command. We've spoken of the principle. The command is to obey God by keeping Him first in our lives.

Trust

Another reason to give of your tithes and offerings is to demonstrate that you trust God. Trust and faith are inseparable. If you have faith in someone, you will trust him or her. Trust plays a major role in practicing the principle of tithing. Will I trust God to really supply my needs and make provision for my life?

Obedience is an expression of submission and trust. It's easier to obey someone you have confidence in than someone you don't.

Some people struggle with tithing because at the bottom of it all they just don't trust God to do what He has said He would do. Because of this lack of trust, they convince themselves that they must take things into their own hands. That kind of faithless self-reliance cuts a believer off from the supernatural help God would have gladly provided—in His own time, and in His own way.

Stewardship

I give because I am a *steward*: one who has been entrusted with the riches of another. I give back to God in recognition of the fact that He owns everything, and in recognition of the stewardship that has been entrusted into my care. By giving, I'm reminded once again that I really don't own anything.

But I don't just want to be a steward; I want to be a *good* steward. I want to work for the *increase* of that which has been given into my care. And giving helps me remember the whole reason God has left resources in my care at all: to see the work of His kingdom advanced on this earth.

Giving helps me remember that it's not about me.

It's all about eternity.

Faithfulness

We need to develop an unshakeable confidence in the character and nature of a faithful God. Regardless of the physical circumstances, that kind of confidence will get the believer through whatever he or she may face.

I tithe because I have confidence in God's faithfulness. Over and over again, God has proven Himself to my family and me. I have no doubt that I'm much farther ahead in every way because I've put God first in my finances.

And because God has been faithful to me, I want to be faithful in turn. I want to be the kind of person God can "count on" to do His will, hearing and heeding His voice.

As an act of worship and devotion

"It's impossible to worship without giving," says Christal Clayton.[3] I give of my tithes and offerings as an act of worship, an act of devotion.

There's a strong connection here.

The word *worship* means many things to different people. "Worship" in the contemporary charismatic church is most often a synonym for *praise music*. It's that, but it's so much more, too. We worship what we value, so assigning worth is a very real part of that expression.

Scripture tells us that we actually *become* like that which we worship. (See Hosea 9:10.) That knowledge is both comforting and scary.

Worship is a lifestyle, encompassing all that we do. Seeing it only as an isolated event will rob the Christian of a life lived in front of Jesus and for His glory. (See 1 Corinthians 10:31.) Singing and praising are types of worship, but so are walking in obedience, reading my Bible, loving my family and neighbors, and presenting my tithes and offerings to the Lord.

The goal of the human family is to produce healthy, responsible, and reproducing individuals. As our children mature they grow from dependence to a healthy interdependence; from consuming to contributing, and from taking to giving.

The goal of the church family should be the same: to produce well-rounded, responsible, and reproducing Christians. A healthy human family doesn't shrink back from training a child to grow and teaching their little one how to make difficult choices. Neither should the family of God. We need to love our spiritual children enough to train them in the ways of righteousness.

Developing a proper understanding of money is essential to that equation.

CHAPTER 9

DOES TITHING BRING ME IMMUNITY?

J ESUS DIDN'T PROMISE a carefree life without hardship.

What He promised was that He would be with us.

Suffering and adversity are part of the human condition. It's human nature to avoid all situations and circumstances that cause us discomfort and pain. Sadly enough, some present the gospel as a way of escaping hardship.

"Come to Jesus," they proclaim, "and all your problems will be solved." Receiving Jesus as personal Savior does solve life's biggest problem by far: our sin and separation from a holy God.

But no one ever said that life afterwards would be a sunlit stroll through the tulips.

Adversity, including financial hardship, is a part of the Christian reality. But we don't have to face life alone. Jesus comforts us with these words, "I have told you these things, so that in me you may have peace. In this world you will have trouble. But take heart! I have overcome the world" (John 16:33).

Jesus didn't promise a carefree life without hardship. What He promised was that He would be with us. (See Matthew 28:20.)

And that's even better.

Sent into the storm

Sometimes people misunderstand or misapply the principle of tithing. Regardless of their personal conduct, they claim supernatural protection from financial concerns and pressures just because they tithe.

It's true; God does promise to bless and provide for His own.

He did not promise immunity from troubles or lean times.

Jesus said that His Father "sends rain on the righteous and the unrighteous" (Matt. 5:45). Obedient, faithful, generous, Spirit-filled Christians get sick, experience financial challenges, and must work through hard times right along with the rest of humanity.

The gospel of Mark tells us that Jesus actually sent His disciples into a storm. But He wasn't sending them where He couldn't sustain them. He told them to go ahead of Him to Bethsaida, a town across the Sea of Galilee. He knew they would be facing danger and adversity, but He also assured them, "I'll see you on the other side." (See Mark 6:45.)

At another time He said, "I am sending you out like sheep among wolves" (Matt. 10:16). Yes, He is still the Good Shepherd who leads us into green pastures by still waters. (See Psalm 23.) But He doesn't eliminate the toil, the tears, or the perils of life here on earth.

Tithing, stewardship, and faith

Tithing must be coupled with both faith and wise stewardship. Even though you give God the ten percent, you must be a good steward and make wise financial decisions with the remainder. Practicing good stewardship means acting upon your faith, not just talking about it. And the apostle James reminds us, "Faith without deeds is useless" (James 2:20).

We can't blame God—or anyone else—when we run up a credit card bill to its limit with no means to pay it off. We can only blame ourselves. Nobody forced us to lay that plastic down on the counter time after time. Practicing good stewardship requires living within your means. The friendly folks at the bank, of course, are all too happy to advance you credit, providing you with the gun and the bullets necessary to shoot yourself. But they are also the first ones to condemn you if you slide into a financial swamp. Banks will not, and cannot, provide safeguards to keep you from overextending yourself. You must build this guardrail for yourself.

Tithing is not magic. Magic is an attempt to bind some greater force, usually malevolent, to do what you want. Frankly, some Christian teaching looks more like magic than sound doctrine, leading people to believe that God is somehow bound or obligated to do their bidding.

God isn't a genie in a bottle. Our relationship with Him doesn't work like that, nor does tithing. In order to experience the rewards of tithing, we must marry it to good stewardship.

Attempting to practice financial magic reduces tithing to a cold "transactional" relationship. "I do this so God must do that." Tithing was never meant to be a mechanical process. We tithe because we want to honor God and recognize His ownership, not to get God to do our bidding.

Relationship, not fear, should be the basis of our faith in God. God loves us and desires to bless us. As Ron Mehl, one of my favorite authors once said, "If you want to be blessed, be blessable." Being a good steward puts you in a place where God can bless you.

The value of hardship

Those who follow God with a whole heart will encounter adversity, just like everyone else who inhabits the planet. But there's a bright side. Adversity brings us face to face with our utter dependence upon God—truly a glorious place to be!

A life of ease can make us lazy and soft. Hardship produces something of eternity in our hearts.

Paul uses many metaphors to describe our need to endure hardship. In one place, he likens the Christian walk to a race, and exhorts us to run with endurance. Run to win, he tells us, not for a prize that perishes, but for the eternal prize of pleasing God. (See 1 Corinthians 9:24–26.)

Paul wanted the believers in Ephesus to realize they were in a ceaseless wrestling match with the dark side. To wage ongoing spiritual warfare, he urged them to use the spiritual weapons provided in God's arsenal. (See 2 Corinthians 10:4–5; Ephesians 6:11–18.)

"Not only so," he writes in Romans 5:3–5, "but we also rejoice in our sufferings, because we know that suffering produces perseverance; perseverance, character; and character, hope. And hope does not disappoint us, because God has poured out his love into our hearts by the Holy Spirit, whom he has given us."

Notice the progression. Suffering accomplishes something beyond mere endurance. The goal is character, and strengthening the believer's hope in the love and goodness of God.

Hardship, then, is inevitable and part of the human condition since man's disobedience in the Garden of Eden. The question is: *How will I respond?* Will I whine and complain, or will I look to the Lord to show me the way to overcome?

One shining example

Our gracious God, who knows very well what a rough road we will face at times in our lives, provided us with a marvelous story in Genesis 37–50. The life story of Joseph, one of the sons of Jacob and a great-grandson of Abraham, presents a stirring example of someone who overcame great hardship. Joseph consistently responded well in the midst of incredibly difficult circumstances. He is perhaps the finest example of a godly steward in the entire Bible, and his life illustrates how faithfulness in the few things opens the door for more responsibility and opportunity.

The favored son of Jacob, himself a man of considerable earthly wealth, Joseph lived the early years of his life on what you might call "Easy Street". Jacob doted upon his favorite son, lavishing upon him special favors characterized by the extravagant coat of many colors. Such treatment did not endear Joseph to his brothers.

When we first meet Joseph, we see him being sent out by his father to search diligently for his brothers, who were tending the sheep in a distant place.

The plot thickens. Motivated by jealousy and hatred, his brothers seized him and sold him into slavery. Incredible injustice! At that point he could have easily given up on life, allowing himself to become cynical and bitter. But Joseph didn't do that. In fact, he served his new Egyptian master with distinction. His diligence and good stewardship earned him respect, and Joseph was given oversight of the entire household.

He served faithfully, only to be betrayed by his master's lustful wife. "Come sleep with me," she purred. He could easily have traded God's plan for his life for a few minutes of pleasure, but his character, an integral component of good stewardship, would not allow him to take advantage of her sexual advances. Instead of winning him points with the boss, however, Joseph's refusal to compromise landed him in hot water.

The spurned woman falsely accused Joseph of attempted rape. Incensed, Potiphar threw Joseph into prison—the very place that would provide his passage to the court of Pharaoh.

Rotting in jail for a crime he didn't commit wasn't Joseph's idea of a good time. But God had a bigger plan. It was through the avenue of the Egyptian prison that Joseph met the man who would bring him to the attention of Pharaoh. Coincidence? Not on your life!

But once again, instead of becoming bitter or twisted, Joseph made the conscious decision to be a steward in his new circumstance. He served with skill and integrity. He chose to embrace hardship and even unfairness and to be a good steward in whatever circumstances he found himself. Although imprisoned unjustly, he once again gained the trust of those over him. And all the while God was working in his life. Joseph would learn lessons and important skills that would set him up for his destiny: to rule next to Pharaoh, saving his family in the process.

Living in North America skews our perception of hardship and pressure. Surrounded by earthly wealth and riches, we may find it very difficult to resist buying into the lie that we "deserve" more— or that God has failed to supply our needs. The venomous snake of materialism bites even the Christian.

Whenever I see a video of a third world country or visit an impoverished nation, I'm always convicted of my selfishness and usually have to rethink my definitions of "want" and "need."

A few years ago my wife and I stopped off in the South Beach area of Florida on our way to Haiti.

Never in my life have I seen so much wealth in such a small area.

We happened to be there during an international boat show and saw a personal yacht on sale for $25,000,000. Within a day we went from the Art Deco district of Miami to mud huts in a squatter's village in Haiti, the poorest nation in the Western hemisphere.

The stark contrast went far beyond the physical circumstances. The people walking the streets of South Florida seemed hollow; dressed in the latest designer clothes, but seemingly empty of emotions and devoid of expression. The people I met in Haiti, on the other hand, were some of the most pleasant, welcoming people I had ever encountered. The believers in particular seemed to glow with a joy of life in the midst of physical poverty. I couldn't help wondering if their economic condition provided them with a clearer view of the riches beyond this world. The hard life in Haiti has produced in many of these Christians something of substance and faith; they had to depend on God daily to provide for their needs.

On my way home I had to ask myself who was truly wealthy: the economically impoverished Haitians or the worldly rich of Miami?

Gap between sowing and reaping

During the transition between no longer sowing bad seed and beginning to sow good seed, it can be easy to feel as though life and God are unfair.

In my role as pastor I see this gap between sowing and reaping after people have taken dramatic steps to put their spiritual lives in order. They make solid decisions to change their way of thinking and living and begin to sow good seed. The problem arises when they expect their external circumstances to change immediately. Sometimes this happens; often it does not. Yes, the peace and joy of serving God floods the soul of the new believer. But the law of sowing and reaping still holds true.

Farmers understand the gap time between sowing and reaping. The farmers place the seed in the ground during the spring and wait until late summer or early autumn to reap the rewards of their labors.

The same is true in the spiritual realm. There's a gap, a time lapse, between sowing good spiritual seed and reaping the increase. People who come to know Jesus as personal Savior begin making good decisions—perhaps for the first time in their lives, but are still subject to reaping the consequences of previous poor decisions. Unwise, selfish, or rash choices from the past, though forgiven, can still impact a person's life.

What does bad seed look like in practical terms? Consider people's decisions that impact their earning power: not completing high school, making poor investments or no investments, living for today without thought for tomorrow. All of these choices affect a person's ability to make a living and the quality of life here on earth.

Unwise and ill-considered decisions have consequences. Sometimes an individual may find life unhappily limited by poor choices in the past. But there can still be a wonderful harvest! By making difficult choices today these same people can sow good seed for their children. They may not see the rewards of sowing the good, but their children—and even their children's children—can and do.

Even so, the "gap" is troubling.

"I don't understand," people will tell me. "I've decided to live for the Lord, but things in my life just keeping getting worse!"

Their frustration during the transition time can be a reason people give up or seem to have no endurance. For people like me who grew up in a very stable environment, it's easier to hang in there when life takes a hard turn. Why? Because the majority of my experience has shown me that if I just persevere things will get better. For people who have grown up in dysfunction, however, they don't have such assurances to cling to in difficult circumstances. Their experience tells them that if things are bad now, they will only get worse.

During this time between the bad crop and the new crop, people can become discouraged. That's one very good reason why God wants to place people in community. We need to encourage those who are making life-changing decisions not to give up, to hold out until the good crop arrives, as it surely will.

"Let us not become weary in doing good," Paul writes to the Galatians, "for at the proper time we will reap a harvest if we do not give up" (Gal. 6:9).

It Doesn't Help to Complain

The psalmist complains to God in Psalm 73. He ranted that the wicked prospered while the faithful perished. He came close to throwing in the towel when he looked with envy on the evident prosperity of evil men. From his human perspective, they didn't struggle at all. They enjoyed health. They seemed free from the burden of trying to eke out a living, living careless and carefree off the fat of the land.

You've got to appreciate this man's honesty with God. "I have followed You and kept myself pure in vain," he laments. "What has serving You gotten me?"

I see something else in this honest conversation between the psalmist and God. Here was a man who was really trying to live a life that was pleasing to God. He was endeavoring to keep his life pure and righteous. The problem was that he wasn't seeing the fruit of these eternal choices. Where were the results?

What he came to realize was that he had his eyes in the wrong place. When he finally began to see past the mere physical evidence, he was reminded of the moral and spiritual bankruptcy of such lives and their eventual end. How much better it is to put faith and trust in a living God, whose rewards are eternal.

Sources of Opposition

I don't know about you, but I can get into a heap of trouble all by myself—without the devil even showing up. It's all too easy to blame the Evil One for our own rash choices or poor planning.

Don't get me wrong. I know that our adversary's unchanging job description through the millennia has been to rob, cheat, steal, and destroy in all areas of believers' lives. (See John 10:10.)

Even so, Satan isn't the only source of our trouble in life.

Understanding the sources of adversity can help us place the blame where it belongs and respond accordingly.

Satan

No discussion on financial hardship would be complete without mentioning spiritual opposition. Ephesians 6:12 admonishes us to remember that our struggle is not against flesh and blood. This spiritual battle wages hot against anyone who would honor God; and Satan will try to destabilize every area of our lives, including our finances.

Satan stands in opposition to God, His kingdom, and His people. In fact, the very word *Satan* means "adversary". Peter warns, "Be of sober spirit, be on the alert. Your adversary, the devil, prowls about like a roaring lion, seeking someone to devour. But resist him, firm in your faith, knowing that the same experiences of suffering are being accomplished by your brethren who are in the world. And after you have suffered for a little while, the God of all grace, who called you to His eternal glory in Christ, will Himself perfect, confirm, strengthen [and] establish you" (1 Pet. 5:8–10, NAS).

Our own foolishness

Sometimes we need look no further than ourselves for the source of our adversity. I can be my own worst enemy. (See James 1:13–15.) My own disobedience and foolishness can contribute greatly to personal hardship without any direct intervention by anyone, including the devil.

Accepting personal responsibility is part of maturity—both personal and spiritual.

So I find myself in stressful circumstances. I don't like where I am. I don't like what's happening to me. But am I willing to look closely enough at the situation to see what part I may have played in the whole mess?

When faced with any kind of hardship or adversity, we need to take a hard look at the *why*, before we start moaning, "Why me?"

Here are a few questions we might ask ourselves:

- What happened?

- Why did it happen?

- Did I do anything that helped or hindered the outcome?

- Could I have done something differently?

- Why am I feeling this financial pressure?

- Am I living within my means?

- Is the solution to this financial challenge something within my sphere of control?

ᕱ Do I have unrealistic expectations about the level
of God's provision? Am I practicing good stewardship of the resources available to me? Have I done
anything that has contributed to this situation?

ᕱ Do I need to do anything to rectify this situation?

A test from God

The professors in the university I attended had a philosophy of
testing that I loved: tests are to discover what you know, not what
you don't know. If fallen human beings can figure this out, I'm
certain that an all wise and all loving God understands this, too.

God does test people, but He doesn't tempt them. He's not up
in heaven trying to trip us up so that we fail. Nor is He setting
traps to snare us in wrongdoing so that He can disqualify us. Let
me assure you my friend, if God were against us, we would really
be in trouble.

But He's not.

He's *for* us.

God is my friend and not my foe.

Although God doesn't tempt us to do evil, He does, however,
allow certain things to confront us so that we will mature spiritually and learn to trust Him. Pastor Rick Warren says: "Temptation
is the chance to choose what is right and thus strengthen our
character."[1]

James summarized the biblical idea that suffering can produce
something of eternity in the lives of those who respond well.
"Consider it pure joy, my brothers, whenever you face trials of many
kinds, because you know that the testing of your faith develops
perseverance. Perseverance must finish its work so that you may
be mature and complete, not lacking anything" (James 1:2–4).

Trials and how we deal with them reveal the true content of our hearts. I remember hearing noted author James Dobson recount a time when his staff survived an attack on their headquarters by a man with a loaded gun. After the fact, Dr. Dobson proclaimed how proud he was of their response. He likened the situation to squeezing a tube of toothpaste: when pressure is applied, you find out what's on the inside.

How do you recognize a test from God as opposed to an assault of Satan? The answer lies in the fruit of that attack.

A satanic attack has nothing redeeming about it, other than the victory we have once we have passed through to the other side.

If we look carefully enough, a test from God has a silver lining. God will allow things to confront us, to test us. Our response comes as no surprise to Him. He knows what we will do on the basis of His foreknowledge, but *we* need to know what we will do.

Because we live in a fallen world

The key to overcoming hardship, temptation, and adversity is our response. Will we trust God? Will we listen to His voice? Will we be obedient?

This world, so marred by sin, is not the world God created. Because you and I live in this world, hardship and adversity will come our way. Jesus never promised us a rose garden, but He did promise to be with us.

Jesus came so we could be overcomers, to rise above the challenges presented by the fallen condition of this world. He came to bring hope.

No discussion of enduring and growing through hardship would be complete without mentioning Job. Job is probably one of the most referenced characters in all of literature. Who hasn't heard someone refer to himself or herself as a "Job"? People love to see themselves as suffering for righteousness, even when they suffer because of their own disobedience, or just because they live in a fallen world. No other account so clearly addresses human suffering and God's sovereignty.

At one point in his great suffering, Job cried out, "Though he slay me, yet will I trust in him" (Job 13:15, KJV). Job's worship of God was not dependent upon what God did for him, but on the basis of who God was. Some try to equate living a life of apparent ease with godliness and God's blessing. But Job's experience shows us that "bad things" can happen, even to "good people."

Whether a person is blessed financially or not cannot be the mark of God's favor or His disapproval. Even the apostle Paul experienced times of plenty and times of need, yet never wavered in his trust in God. In fact, the hardships he endured were a part of the greater scheme.

God spoke to Ananias at the very beginning of Paul's ministry and prophesied, "This man is my chosen instrument to carry my name before the Gentiles and their kings and before the people of Israel. I will show him how much he must suffer for my name" (Acts 9:15–16).

Jesus taught that someone who would follow Him must be willing to take up his cross. Jesus endured hardship and suffering while on this earth. "A man of sorrows, and acquainted with grief" (Isa. 53:3, KJV). "Who for the joy set before him endured the cross" (Heb 12:2, KJV). A cross is something that you pick up as an act of your will. You're not born with a cross; you voluntarily pick it up.

The cross, then, becomes symbolic of our willingness to put our old, self-nature to death, to say *no* to our selfishness and *yes* to obedience to God. Putting God first in our finances is all about denying instant gratification and ordering our lives in keeping with eternal priorities.

You could argue that becoming a Christian actually *invites* hardship. So why would people in their right minds become followers of Christ if this were the case? Your answer to that question greatly influences the focus and quality of your life.

Recently I had the privilege of speaking at a Bible college chapel. My message was on the cost of following Jesus and the need of surrendering to God so that He can use us beyond our wildest dreams. After my talk one young woman hung back as I was praying with a few other students. Finally she made her way up to me. With tears coursing down her cheeks, she explained her struggle. She loved God and loved to serve in ministry, but she was afraid that "the price was just too high."

She was right about the price being high.

But the Bible has something to say about that, too.

"For our light and momentary troubles are achieving for us an eternal glory that far outweighs them all" (2 Cor. 4:17). Jesus said, "I tell you the truth, no one who has left home or wife or brothers or parents or children for the sake of the Kingdom of God will fail to receive many times as much in this age and, in the age to come, eternal life" (Luke 18:29–30).

God Will Make a Way

When faced with adversity of any kind, I need to see that God is the answer and not the problem. I don't want to blame God for my poor choices or responses.

Even though the conviction of free choice is foundational to my belief system, I struggle to understand the difference between "God allows" and "God causes." Because God is sovereign and all-powerful, He could keep certain hurtful things from happening. Yet sometimes He doesn't.

In any such discussion, I have to keep coming back to my belief in the goodness of God. He alone sees the end from the beginning, and I must trust Him in this. Even when I don't understand, I can rest in His unchanging nature; He wants my very best.

Romans 8:28 brings this assurance. "And we know that in all things God works for the good of those who love him, who have been called according to his purpose." This verse doesn't say that God causes all things, but rather that He causes all things to work together for our eternal best.

First Corinthians 10:13 is another one of those verses people misquote on their way to constructing a faulty theology. Paul writes: "No temptation has seized you except what is common to man. And God is faithful; he will not let you be tempted beyond what you can bear. But when you are tempted, he will also provide a way out so that you can stand up under it."

People often misquote this verse by saying something like, "God will not allow you to be tempted beyond what you can bear." But as my mentor Jerry Cook says, "Finish the verse!" The verse doesn't promise we won't be tempted or tested. What Scripture does promise is that our faithful God will provide a way for us to not only endure it, but to triumph in the midst of the temptation. We need to open our eyes to see the way of escape that God is providing for us.

There once was a man who lived on a flood plain. The television news reported that the area's major river was cresting high above flood stage and instructed everyone to seek higher ground. The man simply said, "I'm trusting God." When the floodwaters arrived, surrounding his house, a sheriff came in a rowboat to rescue the man. Once again, his response was, "I'm trusting God." Within a short time, the waters rose, covering his house completely except for the roof. A helicopter appeared to rescue the man from certain death by drowning. The man again refused help, waving the chopper away. "I'm trusting God!" he shouted.

Soon the floodwaters swept the man to his death. When he arrived at the pearly gates, God met him with open arms. But the recently drowned man had something that troubled him. "God, I was trusting You—and You let me drown!"

Patiently the Father listened. When the man finished God simply said, "I sent a news report, a rowboat, and a helicopter to save you, but you wouldn't listen."

The bottom line? Trust God, but do your part.

CHAPTER 10

HOW SHOULD
WE RESPOND?

So Moses sent a message throughout the camp announcing
that no more donations were needed. Then at last the people
were restrained from bringing more!

—EXODUS 36:4, TLB

WHEN PEOPLE HEAR the word *church*, many different
pictures come to mind.

For some the church is an old stone building in the
middle of town, complete with large wooden doors and stained
glass windows. And what does it house? An antiquated, outmoded
institution with no relevance for the contemporary world.

What image comes to your mind?

When I hear the word *church*, it evokes a sense of awe and love.
I see a picture of something alive, even glorious. I tell people that
I'm in love with two women: my wife and the church. The Holy
Spirit chose the metaphor of a *bride* to communicate a spiritual
truth about the church. And like a bride in love with her husband,
the church should be radiant in the full bloom of her womanhood.
(See Ephesians 5:27.)

The opening chapters of the Book of Acts record the birth of the church and provide the best place to see what she was meant to be. A keen sense of joy and God's presence characterized this community of believers. They loved God, and they loved each other. They took Jesus' Great Commission seriously, and some have estimated that a full quarter of the Roman world had become Christians by A.D. 70.

Vital signs

Then, now, and always, the church is people.

It's not a building, and never has been.

It's not an organization, but a living organism.

The calling of the church remains constant throughout the ages: to represent the Lord Jesus Christ on earth, to be His ambassadors. (See 2 Corinthians 5:20.) As beloved children of God, we are to be the reflection of the Father's love for the fallen world.

Jesus, the master of metaphor, inspired His followers to be salt and light. "You are the salt of the earth. But if the salt loses its saltiness, how can it be made salty again? It is no longer good for anything, except to be thrown out and trampled by men" (Matt. 5:13).

Salt has a saving power and so should we. Jesus encouraged His believers to use this power to make a difference in a world that needed preserving.

He went on with His graphic comparisons, saying, "You are the light of the world. A city on a hill cannot be hidden. Let your light shine before men, that they may see your good deeds and praise your Father in heaven" (Matt. 5:14, 16).

The message of the Gospel is good news for people's finances, too, providing a beacon that shines in the darkness of ignorance and despair, lighting the way to safety.

The Role of the Church

People underestimate—or refuse to admit—the impact and contribution that a healthy church can make on a society. As the church in any given nation truly understands its mandate and mission, it will, in fact, save the civil government countless resources that would normally be poured into social programs. The church will aid men, women, and children who have been crippled by abuse, addiction, neglect, and divorce.

How can you place a dollar figure on health and wholeness, wisdom and joy in thousands of human beings formerly dedicated to serving their own selfish interests? How can you calculate the benefit of a single child who, introduced to Jesus at an early age, shuns self-destructive behavior and a lifestyle that drains the social resources of a community?

Human society is dysfunctional because sin is dysfunctional. Sin causes and perpetuates the cycle of suffering. Throwing money at social challenges is often futile because the social problem is really a reflection of a much greater need, a spiritual one.

Bill Hybels, founding pastor of one of the truly great churches in the world, has said, "The local church is the hope of the world."[1] And for anyone familiar with Willow Creek Community Church in South Barrington, Illinois, the "Acts 2" community there has touched not only Chicago, but also the world. Their infectious message? That the church of Jesus Christ can make an incalculable difference in a broken world.

Every local church is meant to be a place where people who love Jesus band together to make a difference: a channel of God's blessing to the world. (See Ephesians 3:10.)

The church is to be a storehouse where the physical and spiritual needs of people can be met. The early believers plunged themselves into the task of meeting the needs of the whole man, spirit, soul, and body. They understood their calling to be a resource place for believers and non-believers alike.

A look at history shows that most, if not all, of our benevolent services began within the church: hospitals, schools, universities, aid to the poor and the disenfranchised. The generations of believers that have gone before us took Jesus' encouragement seriously; giving someone a cup of cold water in His name would not go unnoticed. (See Matthew 10:42.)

The idea of a social conscience was born in the womb of the church. Care and concern for others is a direct result of a Christian worldview, embracing the concept that every human being is important to God. Contrast this with the godless worldview of the survival of the fittest, where humanity is relegated to the level of animals, governed not by love but by the law of the jungle, where only the strong survive.

A scene from Dickens' *A Christmas Carol* shows how calloused people can be to the plight of others. Some of the local businessmen come to the establishment of Ebenezer Scrooge requesting a donation for the poor and the needy.

"Are there are no prisons?" he responds.[2]

Scrooge bluntly expresses his preference that the poor should die and decrease the surplus population. How different is this attitude from the heart of God that cares for each individual.

What I find ironic is that even people who claim to be atheists talk in terms of moral obligation to help the needy and feed the hungry. What they don't acknowledge is that moral obligation couldn't even exist apart from the revelation of a just and holy God, to whom everyone will one day give an account. Something deep within us tells us that we are, in fact, our brother's keeper.

Jesus had a heart for others and so should we. He felt compassion for the multitudes because they were like sheep without a shepherd. (See Matthew 9:36.) He acknowledged that "the poor you will always have with you" (Matt. 26:11), which only reminds us of our responsibility to our fellow man. We are called to be His hands and feet to do what we can to meet human need of any kind in His name.

We care because He cares.

What's the most important then, meeting people's physical needs or spiritual needs? What is the priority? Some say that the church has the responsibility of feeding the hungry. Others say that everyone will die eventually, and getting people to know Jesus and ensuring their eternity is of utmost importance.

And they are both right.

It has been said that hungry stomachs have no ears. On the other hand, full stomachs can pass into an eternity separated from God.

It's not either/or, but both.

Modeling Good Stewardship

God is not a God of disorder, the apostle Paul wrote, but of peace. (See 1 Corinthians 14:33.) Though he was speaking directly to the orderly exercise of spiritual gifts in this passage, there's an overarching truth here.

God is an orderly God.

God blesses order in all that we do, including our finances and how we do church. Ministry and money are intertwined, and because we live in a physical world, there is no way to untwine them! No matter where you travel across the world, it requires physical and financial resources to spread the gospel and sustain the church. In one country I visited recently, the English-speaking congregations gave 90 percent of the budget needed to reach the rest of the country. Four churches blessed with people who had financial resources made ministry possible in the 800-plus house churches in the outlying countryside.

So how should the contemporary church communicate the spiritual truth of giving in an age of skepticism and materialism? It really isn't all that complicated. Each local church must handle its finances and administration in a responsible way that earns the confidence of the people so its members will give their tithes and offerings. If you can't trust your church with your finances, how can you trust them with your life and your future?

Not only does the local church need to be a good steward, it needs to *appear* to be a good steward. Perception is reality in most cases.

What then would such good stewardship look like?

If a church manages its finances with thoughtful integrity, the trust level within that fellowship would be high. People would have confidence in leaders who are wise and responsible in the use of resources. The leadership would communicate clearly about financial matters, thinking not only about present priorities, but also long-term needs. Responding to financial crises would be an exception, rather than the norm.

The proof of good stewardship would be visible. What about the general repair and condition of the facilities? Does the church pay attention to the details? Does money designated for a specific place or cause only go to the place for which it was collected? Using money collected for a specific purpose, but used in another place of ministry is unethical and dishonest, even if the cause is just. Salaries would be in keeping with the income and size of the church—not too little or too much.

Here are some other ways a local church demonstrates its trustworthiness:

- By functioning within its financial means and not spending more than its income.

- By having accountability structures in place— publishing financial statements and an operating budget annually so people can see how money is spent.

- By being above reproach in all of its financial dealings with those inside and outside of the church. (I've heard it said many times that professing Christians are the most difficult people to do business with. How sad.)

- By not confusing faith with presumption—seeking God's will before entering into a ministry opportunity, not assuming God will automatically respond and provide the needed resources for any and every worthy cause that comes along.

When my wife and I first arrived at Sunshine Hills Church, the attendance was small. Everyone in the fellowship knew everyone else. The ushers were diligent and wanted to make sure that the offering got counted correctly week by week. What they failed to take into consideration was people's need to give confidentially.

In very short order I discovered that the ushers knew what everyone else in the church gave. In fact, if they saw someone give an offering and not put it in an envelope, they would actually make one out—out of a good heart.

It came as a great surprise to some people when they received an income tax receipt at the end of the year, because they thought they had given anonymously. We made a rapid change by putting strict guidelines governing the handling of money in the church.

And giving went up.

Why did this happen? Was it because the people had confidence in the process? Yes. Was it because God could trust us with more? Yes.

Tithing and church membership

Should tithing and supporting the local church be a requirement or a test of loyalty for church membership? Financial commitment is a legitimate yardstick of belonging, and joining means taking ownership in a positive way. You invest and give your time, talents, and money to what you feel is important. As a member of a local church, you enjoy the benefits of that ministry, and you should be contributing to that spiritual resource so it will be there for you and others in the future.

Tithes and offerings are God's plan for supporting His work in a community. As God's co-laborers, we are invited into partnership with Him to see His work expanded here on earth. Although He can do anything, He has chosen to bind Himself to people like you and me who are willing to honor Him with our finances.

If all who called themselves followers of Christ honored Him with their tithes and offerings, there would be more than enough resources to make a large impact in our region, our nation, and our world.

Sadly, this is not the case. How often does a local church or a church organization have to turn down a spiritual opportunity because of a lack of funds, a lack of faith—or both? And how often does a church make a poor decision, on everything from the purchase of inferior equipment to taking shortcuts in a building project, because of limited financial resources? Almost always decisions made in such situations come back to bite those who made them.

As part of my quest to discover what I believe about tithing, I took a close look at the written material our local church has produced over the years regarding membership. On our membership application I noticed that the only responsibility mentioned specifically on the application was "I promise to support the church with my tithes and offerings."

Even though it was never our intent, this appeared to communicate an overemphasis on finances, confirming the suspicions of those who feel that "the church is only interested in my money." We rewrote the membership application for our church to read, "I promise to support the church spiritually by practicing my spiritual gifts, physically with my attendance, and financially with my tithes and offerings."

A church cannot go forward without a commitment of the people who attend to support that work in all respects, including, but not limited to, finances.

Whether the exchange is money or goods, the work of God is supported by material contributions. We see this connection throughout the whole Bible. In the Old Testament people brought materials for the construction of the tabernacle. In fact, they demonstrated such a giving heart that the leaders actually had to tell them to stop giving. (See Exodus 36:3–6.)

Wouldn't *that* be refreshing!

What about tax credit?

Most local churches provide envelopes that a contributor can fill out with name, address, and date, so their giving can be tracked and receipted at the end of the year. This practice provides people with a way to give discretely and privately, yet receive an annual income tax receipt.

For some this presents a stumbling block. They cite Jesus' admonition not to let the left hand know what the right hand was doing. (See Matthew 6:3.)

But why did Jesus make these remarks? The offering box at the temple had a kind of metal "trumpet" to receive the money people gave. The funnel, of course, reverberated when coins were dropped into it. This "announced" how much a person was giving—the more the offering, the longer and louder the sound. The overall context of Jesus' teaching here was really about motivation; giving from a heart of love, not so others might see and be impressed.

So giving in a way that can be receipted is simply wise stewardship. Currently governments in North America recognize the value that charities, like churches, do for the good of the society and make tax allowances for giving up to a certain percentage. This discipline provides an additional benefit as well: by getting a record of your giving at the end of the year, you can see objectively whether you have truly practiced the principle of tithing.

Teaching stewardship and tithing

The leadership of the local church should teach stewardship and tithing, even at the risk of making people uncomfortable or angry. How to handle finances should be a regular part of the teaching cycle to equip people to be true followers of Christ, so that church leaders don't have to beg during times of financial crisis. This requires foresight and a commitment to long-range planning, rather than simply "reacting" to situations.

When a serious financial shortfall becomes the reality for church leaders, someone will invariably say, "I guess it's time for the pastor to preach on tithing!"

I argue that addressing the money issue only in times of dire need can actually harden people, instead of encouraging life change in thought and practice. If the only time finances are mentioned is when the local church is feeling the pinch, it's all too easy for people to see it as manipulation—"milking" a crisis, real or perceived, to shame people into giving more.

Spiritual leaders need to do just that—lead. Their example should help people reach an understanding of what good stewardship looks like and how it's to be practiced. If a church experiences financial challenges, *tell the people*, and trust them to think and pray through the issues and come to a good decision. Encourage them to be on their knees in prayer. Drawing people into the process helps them to work through their own responsibility and response to the needs at hand. Trust produces trust and creates an environment where God can work.

Stewardship and hardship

Churches, like people, are not exempt from the ups and downs of financial pressures. The regional economy takes a downturn, faithful supporters of the work move out of the area, and prospects for financial stability in the local church can look pretty grim at times. Since situations such as these are unavoidable, wisdom would urge us to save some of the church's resources in the good times for needs in those inevitable lean times.

As we've already discussed, that's what Joseph did. His faithfulness and stewardship during personal lean times opened the door for God to use him in a very significant way—saving both his family and an entire nation. He applied those same life lessons to store up grain for Pharaoh during the seven years of plenty to carry the nation over during the seven years of famine.

In a similar manner, local churches need to create contingency funds; they should put money aside in the good times to cover things like roofs that don't last forever. Churches, like people, have a tendency to spend for the moment, with little or no thought to future expenses. "We don't have enough to take money out of operating funds to put in a savings account," people will say. "We'll save when we're doing better." Once again, however, good stewardship requires forward thinking and discipline.

In the end such planning will pay off.

Churches, as well as each one of us, also need to learn the secret of being content with the level of God's provision for them in a given season. "But godliness with contentment is great gain. For we brought nothing into the world, and we can take nothing out of it. But if we have food and clothing, we will be content with that" (1 Tim. 6:6–8). Ultimately, it comes down to trusting God to provide the resources to do what He is calling that local church to accomplish. And remember, resources follow vision.

Handcuffing the Almighty?

Could our disobedience and lack of faith actually tie the hands of God? It sounds a bit absurd, doesn't it? How could mere mortals hinder the purposes of an Almighty God?

The church is made up of individuals. What each person does impacts the whole, for good or for bad. On the positive side, one person's gifts and obedience unlocks another's. Students of human behavior call this *synergy*, where the sum is greater than the addition of the individual parts. People working together can accomplish so much more than one person can do alone. On the negative side, one member not functioning can greatly limit what the larger group can do.

The Bible provides us with multiple examples of how the disobedience or unbelief of a few can hinder or keep the larger community from realizing its potential. We saw this in Nehemiah 13, where the people's unwillingness to tithe kept the priests and Levites from doing their assigned tasks in the temple. This, in turn, greatly hindered the spiritual development of the covenant people.

Matthew 13:54–58 records another example of people standing in the way of God's desire to bless. The citizens of Nazareth, the hometown of Jesus, just couldn't accept Him for who He was. They only saw Him as the carpenter's son and took offense at Him. "Who does He think He is, *God?*"

As a matter of fact, yes!

Jesus was and is God, and they missed it. Because of the people's response, "He did not do many miracles there because of their lack of faith" (v. 58).

If we're not careful, we can miss what God wants to do in our lives—and the life of our church family, too.

CHAPTER 11

QUESTIONS AND CONCERNS

S OMEWHERE IN THE process of our pouring out of what we have, God supernaturally intervenes and the ordinary becomes extraordinary.

Have you noticed there always seems to be a gap between what we believe to be true and making it actually work in our lives? People can agree with a teaching in their heart, but putting it into practice is a whole different ball game.

The subject of tithes and offerings and how we are to handle our money and resources is no different. Sometimes all that's needed to close this gap is the freedom to ask questions without fear, and to find someone in leadership willing to take the time to explain things and help us understand.

It's okay to have concerns. These are important, foundational issues that have a bearing on daily life.

Concerns, yes.

Worries, no.

What starts out as a genuine desire to order our lives can quickly turn into crippling anxiety—worry that we won't please God, worry that He will somehow punish or curse us, worry that we can't do what He is asking of us.

Questioning can be good, very good, as long as we don't get to the place where we worship our questions and look for an excuse not to do something we know we should. The questioning process requires a great deal of honesty, a commitment to discovering the truth, and a willingness to adjust how we live to bring our lives into line with God's order.

And that's what this final chapter is all about.

What Are the First Fruits?

If you grew up in church you have heard the term *first fruits* in the context of giving to God. In contemporary language, practicing the principle of giving your first fruits would mean to write your tithe check before you pay any other bills or financial commitments.

This is very close to the meaning of *first fruits* for the ancient Hebrews. The Israelites offered the sacrifice of first fruits as an integral part of their belief and practice to redeem the annual crop. "For the Hebrew, it [the offering of first fruits] was an acknowledgement of stewardship: God owned everything and only asked for a portion in acknowledging this fact."[1]

This offering of the first fruits by the Israelites was an appeal for God to bless the remainder of the crops. As with any true principle, both of these are true today: (1) God owns everything, and (2) by giving of our first fruits before deductions, we ask Him to bless the remainder of our harvest.

Solomon links this practice with a wonderful promise: "Honor the LORD with your wealth, with the firstfruits of all your crops; then your barns will be filled to overflowing, and your vats will brim over with new wine" (Prov. 3:9–10).

For me, embracing the concept of first fruits means I tithe first, from the initial portion of the increase. Our tithe *is* the first fruits.

We give in acknowledgment of God's provision, and in faith that He will bless the rest of the "crop."

Many people tell me that they "don't have enough money left over" after they pay all their bills and meet all their financial obligations. As the comedian Joan Rivers used to say, "Can we talk?"

You know, it's strange how this works. But I have found that if I write my tithe check first, there always seems to be enough to meet all the needs. If I wait and write it after I meet other commitments, there never seems to be enough.

Experience is a great teacher; I only employed the latter technique a few times before I realized my error, and began enjoying the blessing.

What If I Don't Make Enough to Tithe?

The people who tell me they don't make enough money to tithe are often the same people who tell me they don't make enough money to budget. My answer to both of these arguments is the same: the less you make the *more* you need to have a budget, and the *more* you need to tithe. The scarcer the resource, the more careful you must be with it.

Budgeting and tithing are related. Both require decisions about where money will be allocated. The tithe goes to God, the mortgage payment goes to the bank, and the list goes on. The budgeting process forces you to pay attention to what comes in and what goes out. It establishes an order which will bring benefits. Constructing a budget that includes giving both tithes and offerings invites God into the process and clears the way for God to work supernaturally on your behalf in providing for your needs.

In your natural understanding you will never make enough to tithe. Research has shown that a person absorbs a raise within six weeks. It becomes easier to spend a little more here and a little more there, all the while justifying the extra by telling yourself you got a raise. Then you wonder what happened to the extra money. What happened is that your standard of living went up, so that the raise no longer represents a surplus.

I read about a professional financial planner who met with a couple to work out a budget. Their income was about $3,000 a month. After hours of hard work constructing a workable budget, the professional made the observation that, if they could just come up with an additional $200 a month, they could make things work.

Then he kept an appointment with someone who was making $7,000 a month. Guess what? The financial planner came up with the same conclusion: if his clients could just bring in a little more a month, they could have a workable budget.

That's when it dawned on him. It's not how much people make, but how they decide to spend it.

Unless you're unbelievably wealthy, there will always be pressure on your money, and honoring God with your tithes and offerings will always require a step of faith and obedience. You will find no shortage of places to spend a little extra cash or some crisis that will absorb any surplus. That is why you must make a decision to tithe separate and apart from externals and your desires. This becomes the benchmark from which all other decisions about money are made.

Although the decision to tithe is not about how much you make, it becomes obvious that the more you make, the larger the amount your tithe will be. If you find it hard to tithe $100 on $1,000, what makes you think you'll be able or willing to tithe $1,000 on $10,000?

Good for One, Good for All

The principle of tithing applies to everyone. For most people, if they waited until they had enough money to tithe, they would wait a very long time.

It's not unlike waiting to have children until you can afford them. For most, having children is not an economic decision. If it were, there would be far fewer children in the world! We're not thinking of the financial costs, but of the joy a child brings into our lives. My Grandfather Gardner used to always say, "Every child is born with his own purse."

The principle of tithing applies to everyone, regardless of the amount of income, and points to the character and nature of God. By asking for His people to give a set percentage, God is being fair. A person who gives ten percent of his income is in a position for God to bless, regardless of the dollar amount, be it a hundred or a thousand. God looks at the heart and not the amount.

We've spoken of the widow who gave God all she had—two small coins—and how Jesus responded. In 1 Kings 17, we read about another widow who gave all she had. This woman was God's instrument of provision for Elijah during a famine. She had limited material resources, just a little bit of oil and flour. Before the man of God came along, she had intended to make one last meal, and then her food supply would be exhausted. She and her son would die of starvation. In response to a directive by the Spirit of God, however, she made Elijah something to eat from what little she had.

She gave first, and God gave the increase.

The Bible says that the jar of flour and the cruse of oil did not fail throughout the whole famine. She gave her little, and God gave and gave and gave.

I have often meditated on this story. I think that each day she would shake out what appeared to be the last bit of flour and pour what looked to be the last drop of oil, only to find the same amount in those containers the next day. This would have required faith and trust in the continuing provision of God for her and her son.

The Fairness of Ten Percent

The very idea of the tithe embodies the concept of equality. The church is called to be a community of believers, interconnected and committed to a common purpose: seeing the gospel of Jesus Christ proclaimed in their world. All believers, whether they make $1,000 a month or $10,000, give and invest in the kingdom of God at the same percentage by practicing the principle of tithing.

Everyone gives ten percent, everyone has equal say. Now I acknowledge that the church is not a democracy, but you get the point. The fact that one person's ten percent is larger than someone else's should not give that person greater influence.

We are not to show favoritism, period. Everyone, regardless of material wealth, has value and is a contributing member of the community of believers. Sadly, this is not always the practice of the church. Human nature once again rears its ugly head, and people who give more money tend to have more influence.

Those in leadership must constantly guard their hearts and actions against the temptation to treat people of financial means differently. The apostle James warned about this type of favoritism in his New Testament letter. (See James 2:1–9.)

"Them That Has, Gets"

Growing up in Ohio, I often heard this expression, "Them that has, gets." In our fallen world those who "have" in a material sense do enjoy an advantage, in many cases, and seem to be the ones who get all the breaks. Material wealth opens doors in the natural realm to things such as education or business opportunity.

The old adage "It takes money to make money" is true in the world system. If you look at many of the people who have been able to make a lot of money in our world, it's because they've had the money to take risks and invest.

It would be so unfair if this was also the case in the kingdom of God, but it isn't. The blessings and purposes of God are not based upon socio-economic status. Any person who practices the principle of tithing can expect the same reward as one who also practices the principle of tithing but may give a greater monetary amount.

To keep this in balance we must remember that we don't always receive in kind, or in monetary ways. God is God and knows what we need. He has an individual plan for each life because we are all unique individuals. Our responsibility is to serve God in the circumstances in which we find ourselves and trust Him with the rest. His responsibility is to provide.

Although financial resources are an earthly advantage, they can also be a tremendous stumbling block when people limit their faith only to the material world and fail to trust in the Lord.

The Time Factor

One of the questions I'm often asked as a pastor is, "Do I have time to get my financial house in order before I begin tithing?"

The more traditional answer is cut and dry. "No, begin tithing right now and see God work on your behalf."

Ideally, I agree with this.

If you wait to tithe until you have a lot of extra cash floating around, you will probably wait a very long time.

On the one hand, as I've already said, tithing isn't magic. Just because you give your tithes and offerings does not mean you will suddenly have a lot more money. Giving and tithing must be married to good stewardship, and this process can take time.

When people come to the Lord, we make allowances for them, giving them time to bring their lives in line with God's desires. Why not with money? Grace must apply here as well. Even so, this must not be an excuse for avoiding what should be done.

Part of the time component is the process of changing our way of thinking. It takes time and a conscious effort to reorganize a worldly financial mind-set to a mind-set shaped by a godly view of money and resources. To make this monumental shift, a person must be brutally honest when taking a look at his or her present situation. The human tendency is to protect one's current standard of living or, in the case of financial chaos, to live in denial and continue full speed towards the precipice of financial ruin.

Being honest with yourself requires a commitment to honor God—with no loopholes. This type of honesty usually requires accountability to someone we trust, who will help us "listen to ourselves." Accountability is not about creating an unhealthy dependence on someone else; accountability is all about responsible self-management.

On the other hand, faith and obedience in the area of finances does open up a door in our lives for God to intervene supernaturally in ways beyond our control. I believe that God can and will meet people in their needs as they move to bring their finances and their lives into line with His priorities. He does provide for us in ways we couldn't anticipate or imagine.

At some point (and it will never be clear-cut or easy), you must make a commitment to being obedient by honoring God with your financial resources and step out in faith.

When did the water become wine? Somewhere between the pouring out in faith and when it hit the bottom of the jars. (See John 2:7–9.) When did the water become solid under Peter's feet? When he stepped out of the boat. (See Matthew 14:29.) The same holds true with any form of obedience that requires action on our part. Somewhere in the process of our pouring out of what we have, God supernaturally intervenes and the ordinary becomes extraordinary. As we step out of our boat of fear and doubt, God makes the "water" solid beneath our feet.

A Place to Start

As the Chinese philosopher once said, the journey of a thousand miles begins with the first step. But just like untangling a ball of yarn, you need to take a hard look at the present reality and develop a plan to unravel the knotted mass in front of you. Here are some suggestions to begin this process:

- Believe that God is a good God who can not only supply your needs, but *wants* to do so.

- Sit down (with your spouse if you're married) and assess your current financial situation, getting it down on paper.

- Decide to create a budget, and make the commitment to keeping it. Also make a commitment to regular, proportionate giving. This moves you beyond the "I'll give when I can" mentality. If your spouse is not in agreement, you're still responsible for what comes to you—the money you make on your own. Instead of making this a bone of contention, why not put God to the test? Suggest that you tithe on *your* income, and then watch together how God begins to work.

ẟ   If you have some fixed expenses like a mortgage or loan payments that make it seem impossible to give a full tithe, make a commitment to a fixed percentage and stick with this amount, regardless of what may come up.

ẟ   If you find yourself with unexpected expenses, make the adjustments somewhere other than what you're giving to God. This again holds you true to your priorities and provides a place for faith.

ẟ   Set a target for reaching the full ten percent. Put a date on this goal. If you just don't think you can tithe a full ten percent, make a decision to give a set amount or percentage—five percent, six percent.

ẟ   Be accountable to someone so that you make progress toward your stated goal.

ẟ   In about three months, sit down and take another look at your financial picture. You will be surprised at how God has met your needs.

ẟ   If you need help in this process, talk to someone in a position of spiritual leadership who understands the principle of tithing and giving.

Creating a Budget

A budget is like a roadmap that says, "This is where I want to go with my finances." Decisions to spend or not to spend are made on the basis of this roadmap. The question, "Can I afford this?" should always be front and center. Without such a budget, you won't be able to follow through on a commitment to tithe and honor God with your resources.*

A budget helps you answer the question, "Am I spending my money wisely, and do my spending habits reflect my new priorities as a child of God?" Just as when you're on a trip, unexpected delays and detours will occur, but the roadmap helps you get to your desired destination.

Just a few budget basics:

§ First make a list of all sources of income. Know the difference between your gross (total) income and your net income (after taxes and payroll deductions). Your net income is the figure you will need to work with in setting your budget.

§ Then make a list of all your fixed and recurring expenses: housing, utilities, food, clothing, education, cars, loans, insurance, gifts, entertainment, and so on. Most people have no idea how much they spend on these basics. If this applies to you, begin by keeping track of every dime you spend for a period of several months. Be prepared to be shocked by how

---

* Many excellent books exist on the market. I suggest that you go to the local bookstore or library and read up on the subject. Often free resources exist in the community that will help put together a budget.

much money you "waste" on little treats that are nice but unnecessary. Spending money on little things that bring joy to life is okay—but not if you can't afford them! In the end, financial pressure or living outside of God's blessing for your life will rob you of any joy you might derive from such little pleasures.

§ Once you have established your net income and your fixed expenses, start putting a budget together. Set a target for tithing the full ten percent as part of the budgeting process. In the early stages of budgeting, you will need to review and adjust it until it's both workable and realistic.

§ Remember, a budget is only as good as your commitment to keep it. A good budget is both realistic and workable. And once in place, it takes discipline to keep the budget.

§ Bathe this whole endeavor in prayer. As with anything that you do to bring your life into order, you will encounter spiritual opposition. In fact, it would be a great idea to enlist others to pray with you during this transition and help keep you on track. Remember, God helps those who honor Him.

Counting the Cost

All of us, at one time or another, have asked the question, "Was it really worth it?" Was the dinner we just paid dearly for at a restaurant worth the price? How about the movie? The new car? The vacation? Did we receive value for the time, effort, or money that we invested? Were there some surprise benefits that we didn't expect?

Following God does have a price tag. Jesus said, "If anyone comes to me and does not hate his father and mother, his wife and children, his brothers and sisters—yes, even his own life—he cannot be my disciple. And anyone who does not carry his cross and follow me cannot be my disciple" (Luke 14:26–27).

We know that we're not to hate anyone. This is one of those places where the obvious and literal interpretation of the Scripture cannot be correct. The original hearers would have had no problem with what Jesus said, because they understood the "conscious exaggeration" that was so much a part of their language and culture. Jesus drove home the cost of following Him by saying that disciples' love for God must be so strong that, by contrast, they would "hate" those closest to them.

Another part of the cost of discipleship is "dying to self." Following Jesus costs us our very life. We no longer live to fulfill our selfish desires. Paul said, "I die daily." (See 1 Corinthians 15:31, KJV.) He understood that only by dying to his old life could he, or anyone for that matter, walk in the power of the new life Jesus promised. We can only experience resurrection by way of the cross.

Luke 14:28–33 immediately follows Jesus' words about the price of discipleship, and records two stories on counting the cost. Before starting a tower, the builder calculates the total investment. Running out of money before completing it would be a huge embarrassment. The next story speaks of a king preparing for war. Before the first soldier marches the first step, the king must count the cost to see if he has the resources to win. If he doesn't, he needs to seek terms for peace.

Jesus ends these stories with these words: "In the same way, any of you who does not give up everything he has cannot be my disciple" (Luke 14:33).

Yes, being a disciple has a cost, but it also has rewards.

Years ago my father purchased an old lawnmower for my brother and me, and we set up a small lawnmoving business. I received a whole $1.50 for each lawn—and really thought I was "in the money." I remember having a special envelope where I kept my money, and I would take great pleasure in counting the crisp dollar bills. This would always bring to mind the old Gospel song I grew up with, "Count Your Blessings," that encourages the believer to enumerate all the wonderful things that God has done.[2]

In the gospel of Luke, Jesus makes a wonderful declaration to His followers.

"I tell you the truth," Jesus said to them, "no one who has left home or wife or brothers or parents or children for the sake of the kingdom of God will fail to receive many times as much in this age and, in the age to come, eternal life." (Luke 18:29–30).

What an encouraging word! Only God Himself could issue a promise that reaches through time right into eternity. But was He saying that God would give back "dollar for dollar" what anyone gives to God?

No. That's not how the kingdom of God works.

God is much more creative than that! In fact, you and I can't even imagine the many ways He is able to bless our lives during our time here on earth.

When was the last time you stopped to remember all that God has done for you? It's so much easier to complain about what we don't have than to be grateful for what God has done for us.

If living a life of peace and fulfillment on earth wasn't enough, those who follow Him have the promise of a life of eternity—

short-term pain for long-term gain. Jesus says, "Give me all of you, and I will give you all of Me." How much more is His "all" than my "all"? Sounds like a pretty good deal to me.

Tithing on the Increase

Once you decide to embrace the principle of tithing, how do you determine the starting point of determining your income, the basis for calculating your tithe? As we discussed in Chapter 4, Malachi 3:8–10 instructed the people to bring the whole tithe into God's storehouse, ten percent of the gross income. This may seem simple for many of you. To determine your gross income, all you need to do is examine your pay slip that tells you in detail what you actually make and where your deductions go.

But for those who are in business, making this determination isn't quite so easy. This introduces something new and very important into the discussion. Should a person tithe on the gross of a business or on the increase, that is, the profit of the business?

My brother-in-law owns a graphics business. He has to buy paper, the raw material needed to do a job. Then he has to pay workers out of the money charged for the job. The payment for the specific job may in fact be $2,000, but the actual profit or increase might only be $500. To be faithful to the principle of tithing on the increase, he would tithe 10 percent of the $500 he gained, and not on the $2,000 payment for the entire job. Tithing on the increase, then, means tithing on the profit of your business, and not on the inventory or overhead costs.

Tithing on the increase might also come into play when selling a house. Do you tithe on the whole amount of the sale, or on the profit? Again, let's take a look at some specifics. People purchase a first house for $150,000. Ten years later they sell that same house for $250,000. Do they tithe on the $250,000 or the $100,000 of profit they made? The principle of tithing on the increase means tithing $10,000 on the $100,000 profit.

In all of these considerations, however, beware of our human tendency to rationalize. Given enough time and motivation, we can convince ourselves that black is gray and gray is white. Rationalization makes excuses and gives reasons for not doing something, when deep down inside we know we should. Rationalization is the enemy of honesty. Make sure that your "starting point" for tithing has been thought through, prayed through, and bounced off of a few of your most trusted accountability partners.

Let's look for ways to give, rather than for excuses to limit our giving.

It's been said many, many times before, but that doesn't make it less true: you can't out-give God.

The Problem of Inflation

People who have made the decision to put God first with their financial resources are not swayed by the changes in the economy, including inflation. A principle is a principle, and it applies regardless of external circumstances.

Growing up, I remember my parents talking about getting a candy for a penny and making 25 cents an hour. Now my kids have to listen to me reminisce about buying a soda pop for five cents and a candy bar for a dime. Things used to cost less, but people made a lot less, too.

The inflationary spiral affects the church world. Twenty-five dollars certainly doesn't go as far as it did in 1960—or 2006, for that matter—yet many people have not adjusted their giving to "keep up with inflation." This isn't a problem for those who embrace the principle of tithing.

Ten percent is ten percent.

For those who have embraced the principle of tithing, inflation doesn't even enter into the decision. A tithe is a tithe, and I believe that God honors His Word in times of plenty and times of want.

In Which Kingdom Do You Live?

A kingdom has a king. Which king are you serving: God or self? Serving God means you're part of the kingdom of light. In serving self, you think you are serving your own desires, but in fact you're operating in the kingdom of darkness.

A man or woman exercises stewardship either in the kingdom of light, where God is King, or the kingdom of darkness, where they think they're serving self, but are actually slaves to the god of this world. (See 2 Corinthians 4:4, NAS.) Those who operate in the kingdom of God see themselves as stewards over all that God has entrusted into their care and for which they will one day be required to give an account. Those who operate in the kingdom of darkness have a very different focus for their stewardship. It's all about them and meeting their own selfish ends.

Jesus told a fascinating story about a man committed to the kingdom of self.

> There was a rich man whose manager [or steward] was accused of wasting his possessions. So he called him in and asked him, "What is this I hear about you? Give an account of your management, because you cannot be manager any longer."
>
> The manager said to himself, "What shall I do now? My master is taking away my job. I'm not strong enough to dig, and I'm ashamed to beg—I know what I'll do so that, when I lose my job here, people will welcome me into their houses."
>
> So he called in each one of his master's debtors. He asked the first, "How much do you owe my master?"
>
> "Eight hundred gallons of olive oil," he replied.

The manager told him, "Take your bill, sit down quickly, and make it four hundred."

Then he asked the second, "And how much do you owe?"

"A thousand bushels of wheat," he replied.

He told him, "Take your bill and make it eight hundred."

The master commended the dishonest manager because he had acted shrewdly. For the people of this world are more shrewd in dealing with their own kind than are the people of the light.

—Luke 16:1–8, niv

The master commended the dishonest manager on his actions. This unrighteous steward knew how to operate in his "kingdom" better than the people of light knew how to operate in theirs. The moral of this story: whatever kingdom you decide to operate in, you had better know how to play that system to the fullest.

Do You Possess Your Possessions?

The unbridled pursuit of acquiring money and earthly wealth soon overtakes a person; they become obsessed or possessed with acquiring more and more. The word *possess* means "to own or have; to control or influence strongly." Do you possess your possessions, or do your possessions hold or control you?

Are your possessions more important to you than people? One of my father's favorite expressions applies here. He always says, "Things are for using; people are for loving." In too many cases we invert this: we love things and use people.

Abraham was a man who possessed his possessions. He understood that God owned everything and he owned nothing. Abraham also understood that this world was not his true home. He saw himself as a sojourner, a man who was looking for the city "whose architect and builder is God" (Heb. 11:10). Because this world was not his permanent home, it helped him keep earthly wealth in perspective.

Not Depending on Egypt

Growing up in church, I picked up many catch phrases that reference a story or stories from the Bible that describe the human condition. One such phrase was "not depending on Egypt."

Biblically, the phrase refers to Israel's tendency to depend upon human kingdoms to get them out of a jam, instead of trusting God to meet their needs. The Israelites did this at key junctures throughout their history. They would try to buy an army instead of believing that God would protect them.

Are we so much different? Our tendency is to look to many different sources instead of putting our faith in a God who not only loves us, but also has the power to *do* something about the challenges we face. Somehow it seems easier to scheme and try to work the angles rather than to have faith—to depend on the resources that we can see instead of having faith in the God we cannot see.

Another lesser-known story from the Bible illustrates the reality of the unseen realm. (See 2 Kings 6:8–17.) The Arameans were at war with the Israelites. As the hostilities continued, Elisha, through divine revelation, would tip off Israel's king of the enemy's military plans. And that, of course, would render them useless. Infuriated, the king of Aram was certain someone was spying on them.

In frustration, the Aramean monarch ordered his army to surround the city of Dothan where Elisha was. When Elisha's servant looked out and saw the enemy army with horses and chariots surrounding the city, he panicked. Elisha, however, wasn't concerned. Why? Because he saw something that his servant did not or could not; the prophet saw into the spiritual realm.

> "Don't be afraid," the prophet answered. "Those who are with us are more than those who are with them." And Elisha prayed, "O LORD, open his eyes so he may see." Then the LORD opened the servant's eyes, and he looked and saw the hills full of horses and chariots of fire all around Elisha.
>
> —2 KINGS 6:16–17

The servant could only depend upon what he saw with his human eyes. Elisha, on the other hand, was not dependent upon human agencies but upon God.

In a similar manner we need to understand that "those who are for us" are greater than all the hosts of hell that would marshal against us. Our first response when faced with an impossible situation should be to turn to God, not depend on our own understanding.

I sometimes find it too easy to put "plan A" into place, which is to depend upon my own resources. Only after this fails do I cry out to God. We need to look to God first. He should be our "plan A" and our only plan.

To Gamble or Not to Gamble...

Gambling is a contemporary example of "looking to Egypt" to meet our needs. People who gamble are yearning for that proverbial "big score" that will erase their financial problems in a heartbeat. What they don't realize is that they exchange one set of problems for another. Gambling is extremely addictive and has ruined the lives of untold numbers of people.

Christians over the last few decades have retreated from earlier hard positions on many things once forbidden, including gambling. This "softening" has been both good and bad. On the good side we have been freed from the repressive legalism that sometimes held the people of the church in a vise. On the bad side we have allowed certain practices to creep into our lives that are not only a distraction, but can be extremely destructive to our Christian walk and witness.

Gambling is one such issue that has wiggled its way into the thoughts of God's people in the name of freedom and "good fun."

The first time I remember being introduced to the concept of gambling was on the school playground. The boys would come with their bag of marbles and play "for keeps." This game of marbles is where you put your marbles into a circle and you shoot with a larger one, trying to knock the marbles out of the circle. The ones you knock out, you keep. It seems innocent enough until you take a hard took at the principle behind what appears to be an innocent game. You risk your marbles to gain more!

Many parents would either have let this slide or would even have been unaware of the possible implications of this playground activity. Not my dad. He was right on the spot when he heard my brother and me talking about what was happening. He helped us see that this was a form of gambling: trying to get something for nothing by risking what you had. And trying to get something for nothing is really a form of stealing.

So is gambling wrong? *Baker's Dictionary of Christian Ethics* defines gambling as "the transfer of something of value from one person to another on the basis of mere chance."[3] Does this sound like an activity in which a follower of God should participate? Doesn't this mean that an individual places his or her faith in chance and luck instead of in God and His provision?

Even strong Christians can inadvertently slip into giving credit to luck instead of to God. When something good happens people say, "Boy, was I lucky." When something bad happens, such as an earthquake or some other natural catastrophe, they refer to it as an "act of God."

My friend Jerry Cook says that if good things are the result of luck and bad things come from the hand of God, let's forget about God and worship "Lucky."

People who get caught up in gambling don't always connect the dots. It surprises me how many people purchase lottery tickets. Playing the lotteries definitely falls under the heading of gambling. Why? Because the purchaser is trying to get something for nothing—or almost nothing.

In the last twenty-five years we have seen the creation of countless lotteries in British Columbia, the province where I reside. Billboards entice the unsuspecting with the prospects of winning the big one. Lineups to purchase tickets greatly multiply when the pot grows to 10 million. The pull of "get rich quick" is too great for many people. It just seems easier to take a chance than to order life in a way that can be blessed.

"What's the harm in playing the lotteries?" people rationalize. First of all it's usually those who can least afford it who look to the lottery to solve their financial woes. The odds of getting hit by lightning are greater than winning the lottery. And when someone does win, it becomes big news. The other side of that news item tells a very different story, one of the countless people who spent grocery money and funds that should have been put to better use.

Before getting too critical of those who do play the lottery or gamble, how often have you and I trusted in human sources or schemes instead of putting our faith in God? Do you see how putting your faith in chance or luck differs from the principle of stewardship expressed throughout the Bible? Stewardship is based upon hard work and dutifully discharging your responsibility to God, not "leaving it to chance."

The real issue and the root problem of gambling is this: In what or in whom are you placing your faith? Are you trusting in God to honor your good stewardship, or are you putting your faith in "Lucky"? As crazy as it sounds, it seems easier to trust in the far-fetched than it does to trust in a good God and be a faithful steward.

In our first year at Sunshine Hills, when we had about fifty people, one of our newest members came to me with a plan. He had purchased a lottery ticket and informed me he had "made a deal with God." His plan was to give God the ten percent and then give $50,000 to everyone attending Sunshine Hills. He was sure that God would honor him in this very generous offer.

As nicely as I could, I tried to explain that God didn't operate like that. Then, in jest but with a grain of seriousness, I told him that maybe God would be more open if he kept the $1 million and gave God the $9 million.

He didn't think that was funny.

And he didn't win.

Conclusion

ONEY, AND HOW we handle it, plays a large role in how we live here on this earth. As we have noted together in these pages, money isn't evil in and of itself. The *place* we give it in our lives, however, can be either a source of great joy and blessing or deep regret.

The choice is ours.

People need instruction in how to live a life that is well ordered and pleasing to God. Leaders are to teach them to obey everything Jesus commanded. (See Matthew 28:20.) God cares about every aspect of our lives because He loves us and wants what's best for us.

God, by His Holy Spirit, is constantly at work to help His followers become more like Him. This means a continual rearrangement of our thought processes and priorities. Nowhere is this more evident than in the way we view money. How we handle our finances and other resources is a type of spiritual weathervane in our lives, revealing our true motives and priorities.

It's really not about money, but about trusting God to provide.

We need a roof over our heads and food in our stomachs. How we go about meeting these legitimate needs says everything about our walk with the living God. Will we trust our own devices, or will we trust Him?

Money is a tool and not an end in itself. As with any tool it needs to be understood, and the person using it needs to employ skill and wisdom.

The essence of this book can be summarized by noting two things:

1. Tithing is a principle, not a commandment.

2. Tithing is not "magic," but needs to be part and parcel of our life as steward during our stay on earth.

God owns everything and has entrusted us with His resources so we can be a blessing.

We honor a principle because we have been convicted of the truth. We tithe as a decision separate and apart from our emotions or the circumstances of the day. A principle is self-evident, and we can see the benefits of putting principles into practice. A commandment is something that we are required to do.

The decision to tithe or not to tithe is just that—a decision. God gave us the precious gift of free choice. Decisions mean that we are required to make a choice. Will we choose wisely?

Jesus said that we are to be in the world and not of the world. (See John 17.) To be "in" the world means that we have to live here, walking the surface of our planet in a physical body, and have physical needs. At the same time, however, we are not to be "of" the world, governed by a fallen world system in rebellion against God.

Will we use money wisely, or will we be controlled and destroyed by its corrupting influence? Money equals power in our world. And power that is not submitted to God only strengthens our pride and the human tendency to play god.

We are all stewards whether we like it or not. The question is: Will you be a good steward?

The Bible says without apology that God is love. Because He is love, He wants to bless us and give us the desires of our heart. He has promised to meet our needs according to His riches in Christ Jesus. We do, however, need to know the difference between a need and a want. This takes great discernment on our part.

Any change has to start somewhere, and change often begins with a change in how we think. For the Christian, this must go beyond mere human reasoning. The things of God do not always make sense to the natural mind. Sometimes we must make a decision based on faith, believing that God's word is true. Once we are convicted of this, we put our decision into action.

I'm not going to tell you that writing that first tithe check will be easy. In fact, it may be very difficult because Satan does not want God's children to do anything that will put them in line for God's blessing. I can tell you that I believe that God's word is true, and that as you honor Him you put yourself in a place where God can "open the windows of heaven." (See 1 Samuel 2:30; Malachi 3:10.)

And He can give you the desires of your heart. (See Psalm 37:4.)

Summaries and Questions

Chapter 1:
A Matter of the Heart

Summing it up

- As Christians, we need to develop a theology of money that is based on what the Bible actually says and not on what others think it says.

- Money can be either a blessing or a curse. It's a blessing if used wisely; it's a curse if misused.

- Money cannot buy happiness. The only place the human heart can find true happiness and fulfillment is in a loving relationship with the Heavenly Father.

- Money is a tool and, as with any tool, we need to understand it and learn to apply it for its maximum use for the kingdom of God.

- Christians must use money, but keep it in its proper place and not allow it to corrupt them or take them captive.

- The real issue is not money, but who is Lord of your life.

Pause for reflection

- How do most people view the subject of money?

- What is the connection between our philosophy (what we believe to be true) of money and our philosophy of life?

- Why do you think many Christian leaders are afraid to address or teach on the subject of money?

- Why do people have such difficulty giving money to the work of the ministry?

- How is money:

  - power in our society

  - spiritual

  - a tool

Chapter 2:
Portrait of a Steward

Summing it up

- Stewardship is to be a way of living and is at the core of a biblical theology of money and finances.

- You're either a faithful steward or an unfaithful steward.

- The practice of tithing must be married to a commitment to stewardship in order to reap the benefits.

Pause for reflection

- What is your definition of a steward?

- How is stewardship to be a way of life?

- Why is the principle of tithing not "magic"?

- ⚶ How do the following biblical qualities apply to your life:

  - ⚶ diligence

  - ⚶ faithfulness, trustworthiness

  - ⚶ hard work

  - ⚶ seeing God as your source

  - ⚶ gratefulness

  - ⚶ giving

CHAPTER 3:
A CLOUD OF WITNESSES

Summing it up

- ⚶ This chapter was all about interviewing witnesses and finding what they had to say about tithing.

- ⚶ The practice of tithing began with Abraham, and this father of the faith passed the principle down to his son and grandson.

- ⚶ Nehemiah and Haggai both had the same message: the people of God were neglecting the "House of the Lord" to pursue their own selfish desires. Because of this, the work of God was greatly weakened.

- ⚶ Next in the dock was Jesus. He endorsed the principle of tithing and pressed even further to encourage a lifestyle of giving.

- ⚶ Finally, we saw how the Apostle Paul modeled a lifestyle of service, while he championed the cause of those who lead the earthly church to receive remuneration for their ministry. Paul instructed those who were blessed with much materially to understand they had for a reason—to be a blessing to others.

Pause for reflection

- ♪ What is the contribution to the practice/principle of tithing by the following people?

    - ♪ Abraham

    - ♪ Jacob

    - ♪ Moses

- ♪ What are the lessons to be learned from the story of Nehemiah in regard to putting God first with our material resources?

- ♪ What was the concern that Haggai expressed to the people of God? Is this happening today?

- ♪ What did Jesus have to say on the subject of tithing?

- ♪ How did Paul carry the concept of putting God first regarding material things beyond the obligation to tithe, for the follower of God to become a cheerful giver?

CHAPTER 4:
The Message of Malachi

Summing it up

- The message of Malachi includes the famous "Will a man rob God?" passage, but the greater message is about putting God first in our lives.

- Malachi, whose Hebrew name means "Messenger," communicates that we can literally rob God by withholding the portion that is His.

- Putting God to "the test" is really about having faith in His provision as we honor Him with our finances.

- When we rob Him, we are really robbing ourselves of God's blessing.

- Prosperity needs to be defined in terms of spiritual values and not monetary gain.

- As we put Him first, God can, and will, give us the desires of our heart because our desires are His desires.

Pause for reflection

- Most people focus solely upon Malachi 3:8–10, but what else did the prophet have to say about putting God first in the chapters that preceded this oft-quoted passage?

- What do you think it means where Malachi declared to the people of God that they were "cursed with a curse?" Is this "active," where God is literally cursing

His people or "passive," where the curse is the natural outgrowth of not being under God's blessing?

ς How would a Christian determine what constitutes "the whole tithe"?

ς Where was the storehouse in the time of Malachi? What would be the "dynamic equivalent" of the storehouse in our current situation?

ς What should the response of the "recognized church" be toward the "para-church" groups? How do you balance the needs of the local church with other Christian groups that are also doing "God's work"?

ς What does "opening the windows of heaven" look like? Can you think of an example from your own life?

ς Can you think of an example of God "rebuking the devourer" from your life?

ς How do you define "prosperity"?

CHAPTER 5:
COMMANDMENT OR PRINCIPLE?

Summing it up

ς We examined the question: "Is a Christian required to tithe?"

ς The view of tithing as a commandment cannot be supported without a reasonable doubt. Jesus did, however, endorse the principle of tithing and said that His followers should practice this expression of putting God first.

ʒ Viewing tithing as a principle instead of as a commandment opens the door to a whole new dimension of understanding. We enter the world of principle thinking—ordering our lives in accordance with inner laws and not external ones.

ʒ Tithing is God's principle for supporting His church here on earth. We give out of conviction that His word is true, not out of emotion or crisis.

Pause for reflection

ʒ What is your default position: Is tithing a commandment or principle? How did you arrive at this default belief on this subject?

ʒ Why is the answer to this question so crucial for each Christian, church, and leader?

ʒ Now that you have read this chapter, how has your understanding about a commandment and a principle changed?

ʒ Agree or disagree: a principle is more binding than a commandment. Why or why not?

ʒ What is the difference between giving from conviction as opposed to responding to crisis?

ʒ How should a New Testament believer view and apply the Old Testament in living the Christian life?

CHAPTER 6:
PRINCIPLES OF THE KINGDOM

Summing it up

- ⸙ Just as there are laws that govern the way the universe works, such as the law of gravity, there exist laws that govern how things work in the spiritual world.

- ⸙ Some of the laws of this kingdom are:

  - ⸙ What you sow you reap.

  - ⸙ Give and it will be given to you.

  - ⸙ God supernaturally multiplies what we give to Him.

  - ⸙ The laborer is worthy of hire.

  - ⸙ Your heart and your treasure are linked.

  - ⸙ Jesus encouraged us to ask the Father for what we need.

  - ⸙ God rewards our faithfulness and increases what we put to use.

Pause for reflection

- ⸙ Every kingdom has a king, and every kingdom has its own laws to live by. What does it mean for you to be a part of God's kingdom and acknowledge Jesus as the king? What would change, or need to change, if Jesus really was king of your life?

- ⸙ How do the principles of the kingdom of God mentioned in this chapter apply to your situation?

- Can you think of other principles or laws of the kingdom of God that might apply to this subject of tithing?

Chapter 7:
Need or Want?

Summing it up

- The line between a need and a want is very blurred in our North American context.

- Our economic system caters to our selfness and consumer mind-set, which is contrary to godly stewardship.

- God, as our loving heavenly Father, desires to provide for us and gives us the desires of our heart as we follow Him.

- We must guard our hearts from the monsters of covetousness, envy, and greed.

- A thankful heart will see God's provision.

Pause for reflection

- How would a person determine the difference between a "need" and a "want"?

- Be honest, do you really believe that God has met your needs? Why or why not? If not, have you played a role in your seeming lack of provision?

- Make a list of what you see as your "needs." Are these in keeping with what God has promised each believer?

ᔑ What are some practical ways that you could cultivate a thankful heart?

CHAPTER 8:
WHY DO WE GIVE?

Summing it up

ᔑ Motives—why we do what we do—are very important.

ᔑ People give for a variety of reasons; some are good, and some are not so good. "Just because" is no longer acceptable. People need help to understand what it means to give freely.

ᔑ The baseline motive for giving to the Lord is our love for Him and our desire to honor Him.

ᔑ Part of growing to maturity is looking beyond just our own needs and seeing those of others.

Pause for reflection

ᔑ What are your motives for following God? For going to church? For giving?

ᔑ Do your serve God from a sense of obligation or love? How would you know the difference?

ᔑ What are some biblical reasons for giving and honoring God through tithes and offerings?

ᔑ How is giving/tithing an act of worship or sacrifice?

ᔑ What is the relationship between growing in spiritual maturity and being a person who gives freely?

Chapter 9:
Does Tithing Bring Me Immunity?

Summing it up

- ᔥ Suffering and adversity are an inevitable part of the human condition.

- ᔥ Tithing and giving of offerings is not some magical talisman to ward off evil. It does not make us immune from financial hardship, nor does it guarantee you will not have adversity.

- ᔥ God is infinitely more concerned with our eternity than our momentary creature comforts while here on earth.

- ᔥ I identified some sources of suffering and hardship:
  1. Satanic opposition
  2. Our own foolishness or disobedience
  3. A test from God
  4. Living in a fallen world

- ᔥ Finally we also looked at the role personal choice and personal responsibility play in this discussion. You're free to choose, but you're not free to choose the consequences of those choices.

Pause for reflection

- ᔥ Why do you think adversity is a part of the human condition?

- ᔥ What are the four sources of adversity and how would a person tell which one or combination would apply to their present circumstances?

⑤ What can the benefits of adversity be when dealt with properly?

⑤ How does a person live within their means? Where would you start?

CHAPTER 10:
HOW SHOULD WE RESPOND?

Summing it up

⑤ The church is not a building or an institution. The church is people.

⑤ God uses people to meet the needs of His church here on earth.

⑤ As Christians, we are called to Christ's ambassadors. We are His hands and feet to touch people in ways that bring life.

⑤ The leadership of local churches needs to teach and model principles of good stewardship and management of their resources.

⑤ We can tie the hands of God by our lack of faith, which can limit what He is able to do to bless us and bless others through us.

Pause for reflection

⑤ What is the central role that God ordained for His earthly church to play on the earth?

⑤ In what ways could the local church model good stewardship for its members and the community?

§ What are some positive ways that the local church and church leadership can teach on the subject of putting God first with their finances?

§ How can we deal with the reality that many people already have a preconceived notion (usually negative) whenever the subject of tithes is mentioned?

§ How does unbelief "tie" or limit the hands of God?

Chapter 11:
Questions and Concerns

Summing it up

§ Tithing is a universal principle and is not contingent on how much you earn.

§ Making the decision to tithe will always be a step of faith.

§ Creating a budget is the place to start. This exercise will force you to discover where your money goes and what is important to you.

§ We need to ask ourselves in which kingdom we are operating: the kingdom of God or the kingdom of this world system. We need to understand the dynamics and principles of God's kingdom and operate within His economy.

§ We need to take a hard look at where we have placed our trust. Are we "trusting in Egypt," or are we trusting in God?

Pause for reflection

- ꝃ How can you become better versed in this subject so you can do what 2 Timothy 2:24–25 says and help people come to the knowledge of the truth?

- ꝃ Do you think that the biblical teaching about tithing is fair? Why or why not?

- ꝃ How would a person build in an accountability factor if they feel they need some time to get their finances in order?

- ꝃ Why do you think many people do not have a personal budget? Why is this important?

- ꝃ What would "depending on Egypt" look like in our present day?

- ꝃ What are your views on gambling? How would you support your position from the Bible?

NOTES

Chapter 1—A Matter of the Heart

1. Diane Sawyer interview with Mel Gibson. ABC News, February 16, 2004.

2. Christal Clayton, *How to Invest Money with God* (Tulsa, OK: Albury Press 1982), 14.

Chapter 2—Portrait of a Steward

1. Rick Warren, *The Purpose Driven Life* (Grand Rapids, MI: Zondervan, 2002), 46.

2. Ibid., 44.

3. Admiral Hyman Rickover, in an interview with James Earl Carter, Jr., as quoted in "Jimmy Carter", *Wikipedia*, http://en.wikipedia.org/wiki/Jimmy_Carter (accessed March 28, 2007).

4. Andrew Carnegie, in an interview with a reporter, as quoted in Tom Hemenway, "Finding a Sense of Surplus," *Permaculture Activist*, no 46, http://www.patternliteracy.com/surplus.html (accessed March 28, 2007).

Chapter 6—Principles of the Kingdom

1. Richard Blanchard, "Fill My Cup, Lord," © 1964 Richard Blanchard, Sacred Songs.

2. Stephen Covey, *Seven Habits of Highly Effective People* (Parsippany, NJ: Simon & Schuster, 1990).

Chapter 8—Why Do We Give?

1. John Wesley, Sermon 50, "The Use of Money", http://en.wikiquote
.org/wiki/John_Wesley (accessed March 28, 2007).
2. Christal Clayton, *Investing Money with God*, 15.
3. Ibid., 44.

Chapter 9—Does Tithing Bring Me Immunity?

1. Warren, *The Purpose Driven Life*, 201.

Chapter 10—How Should We Respond?

1. Bill Hybels quote available online at: http://thinkexist.com/
quotation/the-local-church-is-the-hope-of-the-world-and-its/761846
.html (accessed March 28, 2007).
2. Charles Dickens, *A Christmas Carol in Prose, Being a Ghost Story
of Christmas* (United Kingdom: Chapman and Hall, 1843).

Chapter 11—Questions and Concerns

1. *Interpreter's Dictionary of the Bible*, J. Morgenstern (Nashville, TN:
Abingdon Press, 1962), s.v. "first fruits."
2. Johnson Oatman, Jr. and Edwin O. Excell, "Count Your Blessings."
3. *Baker's Dictionary of Christian Ethics*, ed. Carl F.H. Henry (Grand
Rapids, MI: Baker, 1973), s.v. "gambling."